A SURVEY OF

World Cultures

RUSSIA AND THE FORMER SOVIET REPUBLICS

Ed Brandt

AGS®

THE AUTHOR

Ed Brandt, a special editions editor for the Baltimore Sun, has written three books: *The Last Voyage of the* U.S.S. Pueblo (1969, W. W. Norton), *When Hell Was in Session* (1975, Reader's Digest Press), and *Fifty and Fired* (1987, Mills and Sanderson). Ed is also the author of another AGS product, *You and the Law.*

PHOTO ACKNOWLEDGMENTS

Cover Photograph: Richard L. Chambers, first appeared as cover photograph for the December 1992 issue of the *LEADING EDGE, The Society of Exploration Geophysicists* publication.

Table of Contents: Dr. I. I. Donick

Introduction: The Associated Press, page vii

Chapter 1: A. Kurbatov, Novosti Press Agency: open; The Library of Congress: page 8; Intourist: pages 5, 10; Dr. I. I. Donick: page 9

Chapter 2: Norm Myers: open; Public Broadcasting System: page 19; The Library of Congress: pages 21, 24, 29; V. Khristoforov, TASS News Agency: page 23; Dr. I. I. Donick: page 27; The Associated Press: pages 30, 31, 35, 36, 39, 40, 41, 44; UPI/Bettmann Newsphotos: page 34

Chapter 3: Dr. I. I. Donick: open, pages 63, 64; The Library of Congress: pages 54, 58, 60

Chapter 4: Novosti Press Agency: open; I. Nosov, Novosti Press Agency: page 72; V. Perventsev, Novosti Press Agency: page 73; Dr. I. I. Donick: pages 75, 81, 85; Patricia Lanza: page 76; A. Kurbatov, Novosti Press Agency: page 77; M. Blokhin, TASS News Agency: page 80; Joseph Madeya: page 83

Chapter 5: Dr. I. I. Donick: open, pages 93, 102, 103, 105; Bibliotèque Nationale, Paris, France: page 92; The Associated Press: pages 99, 100;

Chapter 6: Dr. I. I. Donick: open, pages 113, 114, 118, 122, 123, 129, 131, 132, 136, 128; The Associated Press: pages 124, 126 (bottom, left), 126 (top, right), 137, 138

ISBN: 0 - 88671-720-5   Order No. 80372

CONTENTS

Chapter 3: The Former Soviet Republics

Chapter 4: The Arts and Sciences

Chapter 5: Government

Chapter 6: Life Today

INTRODUCTION

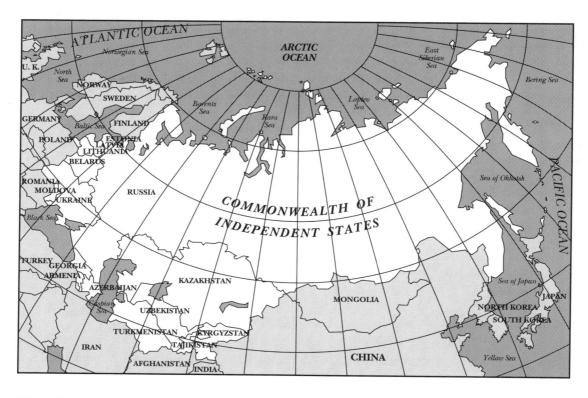

The Commonwealth of Independent States (C.I.S.)

Incredible changes have taken place in the former Union of Soviet Socialist Republics over the past few years. The changes are continuing, and no one knows exactly what the future holds. The turmoil caused by the end of communism in Eastern Europe continues.

For a thousand years, the territory we came to know first as Russia and then as the U.S.S.R. was a tightly controlled society run by a few people. Suddenly, the iron grip of the few has given way to democracy, or government by the people. The former U.S.S.R. shattered into separate parts and the Communist party disappeared into the trash can of history. The changes, and what they mean to the world, are explained in the chapters to follow.

A few of the reasons the former U.S.S.R. was so difficult to control was its vastness and the many **cultures** it included. There were Eskimos in the far northeastern part of the U.S.S.R., **nomads** in the dry southwest, Mongols spread across the **fertile** south, all under the same ruler. There were many languages and many differences in clothing, food, **customs**, and worship. One part really didn't understand or care about the lifestyle of the other.

These cultural differences still exist ·and are an addition to the problems that trouble the Commonwealth of Independent States, a successor of sorts to the U.S.S.R. These problems will also be explored in the chapters to follow.

What is culture? In human terms, it is a pattern of human behavior in thought, speech, activity, beliefs, or something as simple as a tool or ornament created by a particular group of people. For example, why is Christmas an important holiday for many people in the

Ukrainians in Kiev wave their national flag in celebration of independence from the former Soviet Union.

United States, while for most citizens of the Soviet Union it was not?

Christmas is a religious holiday that celebrates the birth of Jesus of Nazareth. In the Soviet Union, worship was discouraged and Christmas existed only for a few. In the Soviet Union, the major holiday was New Year's Day. Gifts were exchanged, and many homes had a small, sparsely decorated tree. This is not to say such a **tradition** will not continue, but now the people of the former Soviet Union have the freedom to celebrate whatever they please.

Christmas is one part of the culture of the United States. New Year's Day as the major holiday was part of the culture of the former Soviet Union.

Holidays are just one cultural difference. There are many cultural differences between the two countries.

The Soviet Union was the largest country in land area on Earth. It was so big that it extended into two **continents**. This vastness had an enormous effect on the culture, or way of life, of the people. The country was so large that it had a wide assortment of geographical and climatic differences.

An example is the republic of Kazakhstan, once the second largest of the Soviet republics behind Russia and now an independent country. Hundreds of years ago, the area was settled by nomadic tribes of Turkish-Mongol origin who wandered from place to place with their herds and their families in search of food and water. Most of Kazakhstan is a **steppe** area, a flat, grassy plain similar to the prairies of the American Midwest. Natural barriers, like mountain ranges, deserts, inland seas, and great rivers, helped to confine the unique Kazakh culture to the steppe. Few nomads now exist in Kazakhstan, but the Kazakh language is still taught in the schools and is part of a culture unlike that of any other.

Climate has a powerful effect on culture. Because of its size, the Soviet Union had vast differences in climate, from the sub-zero chill of Siberia, to the vast, torrid desert of the **Kara Kum** in what is now the independent republic of Turkmenistan. People living under these different climatic conditions eat differently, dress differently, and think differently than people living in other areas.

And there is history, a powerful influence on any culture. In the United States, many place names, like Mississippi, Michigan, and Erie, are a cultural **legacy** of our Native Americans. In the former Soviet Union, the great Mongol invasion of the thirteenth century and the ensuing 400-year rule of the **tsars** set cultural patterns that even the Bolshevik Revolution of 1917 could not change. To understand the culture of your own country and to compare it with the culture of another is an exciting exercise. Why? Because understanding different cultures helps us to understand and get along with the people of other countries. It tells us where we have been, and almost certainly, where we are going.

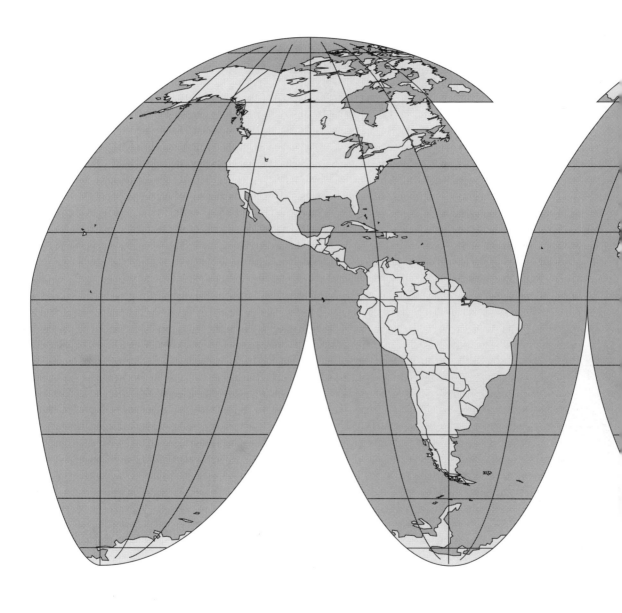

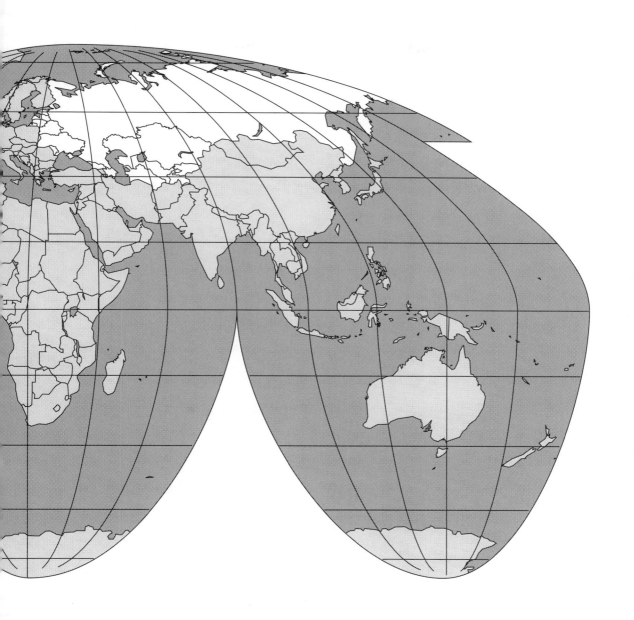

RUSSIA AND THE FORMER SOVIET REPUBLICS

GEOGRAPHY AND CLIMATE

Chapter 1

F
A
C
T
S

- The Soviet Union ceased to exist on December 25, 1991.
- Eleven of the 15 republics later joined in a union called the Commonwealth of Independent States (C.I.S.).
- Russia is by far the largest country in the C.I.S.
- A large part of Russia is above the Arctic Circle.
- The climate of the C.I.S. is mostly cold, dry, and windy.

PART 1:
From the Window of a Train

Imagine that you are taking a long train ride, the longest in the world, more than 5,600 miles across the width of the Commonwealth of Independent States, the former Soviet Union.

At Moscow's busy Yaroslav (yahr uh SLAV) railroad station you would climb aboard the famous Trans-Siberian Express for a seven-day journey through the heart of the C.I.S. (See map on page 14.)

You would travel 950 miles east to the city of Yekaterinburg (ye KAT er in burg), formerly called Sverdlovsk (sferd LAWSK), a city in the Ural Mountains, the boundary between Europe and Asia. Your trip would still be in the early stages. From Yekaterinburg, you would continue east by southeast through the southern part of the C.I.S.

You would travel past Omsk, Tomsk, and Krasnoyarsk before dipping south to the city of Irkutsk

1

(IR kootsk) on the shores of Lake Baikal (by KAHL), its waters still cold and sparkling but growing polluted from the rapid growth of industry on its shores. The lake is the deepest freshwater lake in the world, holding one-fifth of the world's fresh water.

It has been four dizzying days since you boarded the train in Moscow, but you would have almost half the trip to go.

After Irkutsk, your train's path would level out for some miles. Then it would start on a long northeasterly course toward the Chinese border. This is about where the tracks of the Moscow-Beijing Express (it has showers and is cleaner than the Trans-Siberian Express) branch off for the trip to Beijing, the capital of China.

5,630 miles in 7.3 days

From there the train follows the border with China for several hundred miles to Khabarovsk (kuh BAHR uhfsk), and then takes a southerly path to the Russian seaport of Vladivostok (vlad uh vaw STAHK) on the Sea of Japan. Until recently, foreigners were not allowed into Vladivostok because of the large naval base in that city. But under the new attitude of openness in Russia, most of those restrictions have been relaxed.

Vladivostok is the end of the line, at last! A notice on the train informs travelers that the trip was 5,630 miles in 175 hours, or 7.3 days. On this journey you would have seen the real Russia: the people who bustle aboard with battered suitcases, tattered gifts, and toys to occupy their children on the long ride. Although vendors often come through with sandwiches and there are dining cars where meals can be bought, many travelers prefer to bring their own food.

It is the people who make the long trip worthwhile. Bundled in their warm-up suits, families settle down for the long train trip as though they are still at home. They gather in a coach or in a cozy four-to-six-bed compartment. The Russian men play chess, read, and talk while the women sew and tend to the food and the children.

R E V I E W

Directions:
Number your paper from 1 to 4. Answer the following questions.
1. What is the name of the train that goes from Moscow to Beijing? How is it different from the Trans-Siberian Express?
2. How long does it take to travel the length of the Trans-Siberian Express?
3. Why were foreign visitors not allowed into the city of Vladivostok?
4. Who do you think would travel on the Trans-Siberian Express? Why?

SPOTLIGHT
S T O R Y

The Russian Rail System

Railroads have been a powerful force in Russian culture for more than 150 years. Automobiles are not a good choice of transportation for most Russians because they can't afford them, and the road system is poor outside of the major cities.

These are the major reasons there is a highly developed subway system in the largest cities in Russia and other countries in the C.I.S. Russians take great pride in their rail system.

They are especially proud of the Trans-Siberian Railroad, which was once considered one of the wonders of the world. It was begun in 1891 by Tsar Alexander III and finally completed in 1916 during World War I and the reign of Tsar Nicholas II. Hundreds of workers are said to have died from accidents, cold, and disease during its construction because of the bitter **climate** and rough **terrain** of Siberia.

The railroad originally was built to run between the city of Sverdlovsk (now Yekaterinburg), on the boundary between Europe and Asia, to the seaport of Vladivostok in Eastern Russia on the Sea of Japan. An extension was eventually built between Sverdlovsk and Moscow. Today, the Trans-Siberian Express covers the 5,600-plus miles from Moscow and Vladivostok in just over seven days.

The railroad has had a great effect on the growth and wealth of the country, particularly remote Siberia. The railroad opened Siberia up to development and created a highly specialized **elite** working class willing to labor in the harsh climate to develop the industry and trade that sprang up around the tracks. The railroad was a valuable asset during Russia's war with Japan in 1904, and during both world wars, shifting men and supplies across the vast territory.

Since the 1920s, the Trans-Siberian has been joined by other major rail lines, among them the Baikal-Amur Mainline, which parallels the Trans-Siberian Railroad. It was completed in October of 1984. The line connects Lake Baikal with the Amur River in the Russian Far East, a distance of 2,000 miles.

The C.I.S. has the second largest rail network in the world, with about 80,000 miles of track. The United States is first, with about 290,000 miles of track.

Stop and review

Answer the questions below.
1. Why are trains and subways so important to the C.I.S.?
2. Under what tsar was the Trans-Siberian Railway begun?
3. What is the Trans-Siberian Railroad's most western stop?
4. How has the Trans-Siberian Railroad affected Russian growth and history?
5. What country has the largest railroad system in the world?

GEOGRAPHY AND CLIMATE

PART 2:
Largest Union in the World

The long train ride on the Trans-Siberian Railroad would illustrate the mind-bending vastness of the Commonwealth of Independent States, which covers almost one-sixth of the land area of the world. The C.I.S. is an astounding 8 1/4 million square miles of drab **tundra**, dense forest, rich farmland, blistering desert, flat **steppes**, rugged mountain ranges, and mighty rivers. The entire United States plus half of Canada could fit into Siberia alone. The C.I.S. itself is about three times the size of the continental United States and larger than all of South America.

The country includes eleven time zones—the continental United States has four. Moscow, in western Russia, is much closer to New York City in the United States than it is to Vladivostok in eastern Russia. Russia by itself is so large that when the people in Vladivostok are getting up, the people in Moscow in the western part of the country are going to bed. The C.I.S. is more than 6,000 miles from one end to the other. That's twice the distance from New York to San Francisco in the United States.

This vastness has affected the country's history. Because of the many countries that border on it, Russia through the centuries has always feared for its security and has been suspicious of its neighbors, with good reason. The country has been invaded by outside forces from every direction.

A Major Event for Villagers

Many people think of Siberia as a vast land rapidly filling with settlers eager to mine its great mineral wealth. But the view, as seen from a passing train, is of

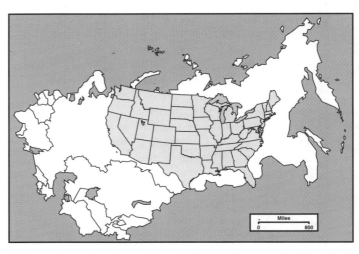

Did you know that the continental United States could fit inside the C.I.S. almost three times?

a sparsely populated, almost empty land. Cities suddenly loom up, only to vanish as quickly as they appeared as the train rolls steadily on into more empty expanse. In between these Siberian cities are small villages where the major event of the day is the passing of the Trans-Siberian Express.

Passengers usually pass the time on the Trans-Siberian Express by reading, sleeping, snacking, playing games, or just talking.

When the train stops, passengers swap goods for food with eager villagers. They pass along the latest gossip from Moscow. Riders also get off to stretch their legs and go to the station kiosk for sweet rolls, beer, and the latest newspapers.

Russians Love to Talk

Russians love to talk, and will talk freely to any foreigner on a long train ride. What would you talk to them about? A tip: they love to talk politics, and they want to hear about America. The United States to many is still a mysterious, somewhat scary land of plenty. They bombard Americans with questions about the United States at every opportunity.

On your train trip, you would have actually seen only a small part of this enormous and **complex** country. Russia is so complex and varied that it is "not a nation, but a world," according to an old Russian saying.

R E V I E W

Directions:
Number your paper from 1 to 3. Answer the following questions.
1. How much larger than the United States is the Commonwealth of Independent States?
2. What are some of the topics a Russian citizen might want to discuss with you? What would you like to ask him or her about?
3. The large number of bordering countries has affected the attitude of Russian leaders toward their neighbors. What might change in the United States if it feared invasion by bordering countries?

PART 3:
Geography of the Region

More than half of the Commonwealth of Independent States is a plain, with gentle, rolling terrain. The union is divided into six main geographical sections. The first is the European Plain (sometimes called the Russian Lowland). This is where three-fourths of the population and most of the industry and best farmland are located.

The second geographical section is the Ural Mountains. The mountains form the dividing line between Europe and Asia. The third section is the Aral-Caspian Lowlands, or what was called Soviet Central Asia. This region makes up the southern part of the C.I.S. The remaining three regions are the West Siberian Plain, the Central Siberian Plateau, and the East Siberian Uplands.

The European Plain

The European Plain has most of the C.I.S.'s population, industry, and rich soil. It also features mighty rivers like the Volga (VAWL guh), Dniester (NEES tuhr), Dnieper (NEE puhr), and Don. The three largest cities in the C.I.S.—Moscow, St. Petersburg (formerly Leningrad) in Russia, and Kiev in the republic of the Ukraine—are in this region of marshy valleys and rolling hills.

The north is heavily wooded, while the south is grassy. The steppes (grassy plains) in the southern part of the C.I.S. are like the flat prairie country in the American Midwest, with few trees, cold winds in the winter, and high temperatures in the summer.

The Ural Mountains

The Ural Mountains, a thousand miles east of Moscow, have an average elevation of about 2,000 feet, small by most standards. However, some peaks in the Urals rise to 5,000 feet. When the Germans invaded the Soviet Union in 1941, the Russians sent much of their industry to the Urals for protection. East of the Urals is the vast land of Siberia. The Urals form the boundary between European (western) Russia and Asian (eastern) Russia. The region has great mineral wealth, much of it still untapped.

The Aral-Caspian Lowlands

The Aral-Caspian Lowlands (the former Soviet Central Asia) in the southwestern part of the C.I.S. has forbidding deserts and grassy **plateaus** in one part, and great mountain ranges on its southern edge. The highest mountain in the entire country is a peak located in the

Pamir Mountains along the Afghanistan and Iranian borders. It is 24,590 feet high. Farther west, the Caucasus Mountain range, which forms the boundary between the C.I.S., Turkey, and Iran, has a number of peaks ranging up to 18,000 feet.

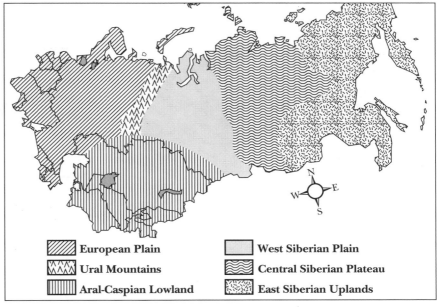

▨ European Plain		▨ West Siberian Plain	
▨ Ural Mountains		▨ Central Siberian Plateau	
▨ Aral-Caspian Lowland		▨ East Siberian Uplands	

Map Study: *This map shows the six land regions of the C.I.S. Which land region is the smallest? Which land region is located the farthest east? the farthest west? the farthest south? Which land region is made up of mountains?*

The West Siberian Plain

The West Siberian Plain is the largest level area in the world. It covers more than one million square miles and its highest point is only 500 feet above sea level. Much of the plain is marshy and not fit for **agriculture**.

The Central Siberian Plateau

The Central Siberian Plateau begins in frozen, swampy coastal plains along the Arctic Ocean and slopes upward as it goes toward the south. The average elevation is between 2,000 and 3,000 feet. It is a region of dense forests and many streams. Some of these streams flow through great canyons and ravines. This region has a wide variety of mineral deposits.

The East Siberian Uplands

The East Siberian Uplands is mostly a wilderness of mountains and valleys cut by large rivers. At its eastern end on the Pacific Ocean are more than 20 active volcanoes.

Frozen Siberia

Siberia makes up three of the six land regions of the C.I.S. and is a large part of the Commonwealth. It is a difficult place to live because of the harsh

This convict village in Siberia housed prisoners at the turn of the century.

climate. For hundreds of years, Russian rulers sent their enemies into **exile** in Siberia. Maxim Gorky, the great Russian writer of the late nineteenth and early twentieth centuries, called it a "land of death and chains." While Gorky's description is no longer true, Siberia is still not a favored place, especially for the young. Its isolation and severe climate make it difficult to keep workers there. The government pays extra money to encourage people to stay.

Names

Russia.

Union of Soviet Socialist Republics.

Commonwealth of Independent States.

This is the succession of names used to describe the vast area you are reading about in this book.

Russia, with a history going back to the ninth century, offcially became the Union of Soviet Socialist Republics (U.S.S.R.) in 1922, five years after the Bolshevik party under V. I. Lenin seized control of the government.

The U.S.S.R., also known as the Soviet Union, existed until December 25, 1991. It was dissolved and 11 of its 15 states agreed to join together in a union called the Commonwealth of Independent States.

R
E
V
I
E
W

Directions:

Number your paper from 1 to 4. Answer the following questions.

1. What is it about Siberia that makes it an undesirable place to live?
2. Where is the highest mountain in the C.I.S. located?
3. Which geographical section of the C.I.S. has the largest population? Why?
4. Which mountain range acts as a natural border between European and Asian Russia?

PART 4:
Bodies of Water and Climate

The Lena River in Siberia flows for more than 2,600 miles and is the longest river entirely in Russia. Other long rivers in Siberia include the Amur and the Ob. They are frozen for seven to nine months a year.

The Volga is the longest river in Europe and is frozen for about three months of the year. It flows from near Moscow to the Caspian Sea, a total of about 2,200 miles.

Russia before 1917 had only a few poor roads. When they were not frozen over, the rivers provided a way to transport goods and people. The road system has since been greatly improved, and air travel is also important to the country. But the rivers are still heavily used for transportation. They are also the source of much Russian folklore.

The Largest Lake in Europe

Lake Ladoga, north of Moscow and between Russia and Finland, covers 6,835 square miles and is the largest lake entirely in Europe. During the Russian-Finnish winter war of 1940, Russian troops attacked Finland across the thick ice of Lake Ladoga.

The World's Deepest Lake

Lake Baikal in Siberia is the deepest freshwater lake in the world. It has an average depth of 5,315 feet. Under the careless government of the Communist party in the Soviet Union, the lake became increasingly polluted by the industry on its shores. Now, efforts are being made to clean it up.

An Inland Sea

The Caspian Sea is the world's largest inland body of water. It covers 143,630 square miles in the southern part of the C.I.S. Russia has fought its enemies for centuries on and around the Caspian Sea, and its shores have been the scene of countless bloody battles.

The Neva River flows through St. Petersburg, a beautiful Russian city known as the "Venice of the North."

Coastline of the C.I.S.

The Commonwealth of Independent States has the longest coastline in the world — more than 25,000 miles. Only a small part of it is usable, however.

Most of the northern waters are frozen or fogbound most of the year, or the waters are too shallow to be of much use.

The only port on the Arctic coast that is ice-free year-round is Murmansk. Even though this city is only 200 miles from the Arctic Circle, the warm Gulf Stream currents from the Atlantic Ocean help to keep it free of ice.

A Cold, Dry Climate

The climate of the Commonwealth of Independent States is mostly cold, windy, and somewhat dry. In contrast, much of the United States is in the temperate zone, which means that the temperature here is much milder than in the C.I.S. The United States also gets more rain than the C.I.S.

The main thing to remember about the climate in the C.I.S. is that most of the Commonwealth is in the north, and a large portion of Russia is north of the Arctic Circle. Some parts of Russia are only 150 miles from the North Pole.

Snow remains on the fields and in the forests longer because of the cold climate. More than half of Russia is covered by snow for more than six months of the year. Almost half of Russia has **permafrost**, meaning permanently frozen subsoil. During even the hottest summer, where there are no trees the soil remains frozen below 18 inches. In the forests, it remains frozen below six feet.

The most southerly point in Russia is at the 36th Parallel, which is about the same parallel as Oklahoma City, Oklahoma, in the United States. Oklahoma City has a moderate climate.

The warmest area year-round in the C.I.S. is the Crimean coast on the northeastern shores of the Black Sea. This is a popular vacation spot for many Russians. The area has a Mediterranean climate, with warm temperatures, dry summers and rainy winters.

Yalta is a popular Russian resort on the Black Sea. Vacationers there can enjoy lunch in the splendor of the Swallows Nest Castle.

Around most of the rest of the country, winters are long, cold, and windy and last from October to late April. In Siberia, temperatures have dropped to a world record 96 degrees Fahrenheit below zero. Temperatures of 45 degrees below zero are not unusual in Moscow.

Summers Are Short

Summers are short, windy, hot, and dry. This is why Russia and other C.I.S. republics have trouble growing crops. The average growing season is 120 to 160 days. The United States has a much more favorable growing season. It ranges from 150 to 260 days. In some places, like California and Florida, crops are grown year-round. In addition, less rain and snow falls on the C.I.S. than on the United States. Large parts of the C.I.S. are **arid**. Other parts have low yearly rainfall and depend on **irrigation** to raise crops.

The average yearly rainfall in the northwestern areas of the C.I.S., where many crops are grown, is 25 inches. In contrast, the state of Maryland in the United States averages about 41 inches of rain a year. Farther south in the C.I.S., around the Caspian Sea, only 4 to 8 inches of rain fall a year. Much of this area is desert.

The Soviet Union, which existed from 1922 to December of 1991, had many crop failures because of low precipitation. In the 1920s and '30s this led to terrible famines in which millions of people died of hunger.

More recently, because of crop failures the Soviet Union was forced to buy a lot of grain from other countries, including the United States.

R E V I E W

Directions:
Number your paper from 1 to 5. Answer the following questions.
1. How have rivers been important to the development of Russia, the Soviet Union, and the C.I.S.?
2. What city in the United States would be at about the most southerly latitude in the C.I.S.?
3. What are three important differences in the climates of the C.I.S. and the United States?
4. How has climate affected the country's ability to feed its people?
5. How important is climate when determining where you are going to live?

PART 5:
The Five Vegetative Zones

The Commonwealth of Independent States has five vegetative zones that stretch in wide bands across Europe and Asia. These vegetative zones are the tundra, **taiga**, steppe, desert, and Mediterranean.

The Frigid Tundra

Part of the permafrost area along the Arctic coast, about 15 percent of the entire Commonwealth, is known as the tundra. The tundra is made up mostly of **bogs** and marshes that are frozen in winter and infested with huge mosquitoes in summer. Vegetation in the tundra is sparse because of the harsh winters and thin soil. The land is bare of trees and the main plant growth in the northern tundra is moss. Berry bushes, wildflowers, and a few trees grow in the southern part. From late September to the end of March the sun does not rise above the horizon. The few people who live on the tundra make their living by fishing, hunting, and herding reindeer.

The Mysterious Taiga

South of the tundra is the taiga, a Russian word meaning "forest." The taiga is dark and mysterious, with dense forests of spruce, fir, and cedar. Farther south are forests of oak, linden, elm, birch, and aspen. There are so many birch trees in the country that it has been proclaimed the national tree. The taiga is almost all forest.

Along the edges of these great forests of the taiga live wolves, bear, squirrel, beaver, sable, lynx, fox, ermine (a type of weasel), and elk. Many of these are valuable fur-bearing animals that have been trapped and sold for centuries. Today there are numerous fur farms in the taiga on which many of these fur-bearing animals are raised.

The taiga also has great mineral wealth: oil, gold, iron. However, few people live in this part of the country and the mineral wealth remains largely unrecovered. The population density is rarely higher than four persons a square mile. Most of these are lumberers, fishers, and hunters.

The Steppe and the Richest Soil in the World

South of the taiga is the steppe, or prairie. The countryside is bare and flat, with few trees. This is due to a lack of rainfall and high winds. Most of the steppe has the richest soil in the world. This deep, crumbly dirt is called **chernozem** (black soil). It can grow crops such as wheat, oats, barley, rye, corn, and tobacco. However, irrigation is needed in much of the steppe.

The rich soil has been a lure for invaders from the earliest times. Yet the steppe continues to be difficult to **cultivate** because of the drying winds and lack of rain.

The Desert

Just south of the steppe is an area that is mostly desert and some semi-desert. Although fewer than eight inches of rain falls on this land in a year, irrigation has transformed millions of acres into productive farmland. Much of this land is suitable for growing cotton, vegetables, and fruit.

The Mediterranean

The Mediterranean is by far the smallest vegetation zone in the Commonwealth. It is on the shores of the Black Sea. The hot, dry summers and rainy winters are perfect for growing olives, grapes, and citrus fruits. There are several resorts in this area because of the mild climate.

R
E
V
I
E
W

Directions:
Number your paper from 1 to 5. Answer the following questions.
1. What is Russia's national tree?
2. In which of the five vegetative zones would you like to live? Why?
3. What is irrigation? Why is it important to farming on the steppes.?
4. Describe the tundra. Why do so few people live there?
5. How does the vegetation or climate of an area affect the desirability of living there?

GEOGRAPHY AND CLIMATE

MAP SKILLS

THE TRANS-SIBERIAN RAILROAD

Directions:

Number your paper from 1 to 10. Use the map on this page to help you answer the following questions.

1. What city is located at the western end of the Trans-Siberian Railroad?
2. How many miles east of Novosibirsk is Krasnoyarsk?
3. Near what body of water is Vladivostok located?
4. If you were taking the Trans-Siberian Railroad from Kazan to Khabarovsk, what city would you pass through first?

5. How many miles is Kazan from Omsk?
6. Of all the cities shown on the map that are served by the Trans-Siberian Railroad, what city is closest to Mongolia?
7. What direction would the train travel to take passengers from Omsk to Svobodnyy?
8. What city shown on the map is closest to Moscow?
9. What direction would the train travel to take passengers from Vladivostok to Moscow?

CHAPTER 1 REVIEW

Summary of Geography and Climate

Taking a train ride on the Trans-Siberian Railroad through the heart of the Commonwealth of Independent States would bring past your window the glories of an immense area. It would also reveal to you some of the character of its diverse people.

Russia alone measures about 6,000 miles from its western border to its eastern border. Within its borders is a wide variety of climate, from the frozen land of eastern Siberia to the hot, arid plains of some parts of southwestern Russia.

Wild game abounds in the dense forests of Siberia. Beneath the permafrost of the desolate tundra, mineral wealth still waits to be mined.

More than half of the Commonwealth is flat land, broken by gently rolling hills. Much of the C.I.S. is in the northern latitudes. Almost half of the Commonwealth has permanently frozen soil.

Critical Thinking Skills

Directions: Give some serious thought to the questions below. Be sure to answer in complete sentences.

1. If you were riding in a train compartment with a Russian family, what are some of the things you would like to learn from them? List the topics that you would discuss separately with the father, mother, and children.

2. Why is the Trans-Siberian Railroad an important unifying factor in the Commonwealth?

3. Why are rivers so important to the people and the economy?

4. There are few luxuries in the Commonwealth. Relatively few people own automobiles, and there is little living space for individual families. The country is rich in mineral wealth and has some good farmland, yet its people still suffer many hardships. Why do you think this is so?

5. Why is the European Plain such an important region of Russia?

For Discussion

Directions: Discuss these questions with your classmates. Appoint one class member to write the ideas you discover on the board.

1. Of all the different parts of the Commonwealth of Independent States described in this chapter, which part would you most like to visit. Why? Where would you least like to visit? Why? Take a poll of the class and write the results on the board.

2. If you were visiting Siberia, what type of clothing would you take along to protect yourself from the weather?

3. Siberia is a mysterious land of dense forests, bitter cold, wild game, and few people. Try to imagine that you are going to Siberia for a visit. What would you most like to see on this visit?

Write It!

Directions: Imagine that you are riding on the Trans-Siberian Railroad. Keep a diary of your experiences. What did you see? To whom did you talk? What were your impressions of the landscape, the train, and your fellow passengers? Begin in Moscow and travel eastward. Be sure to make at least one entry for every day you are on the train.

For You to Do

Directions: Select a city or region in the Commonwealth that you would like to visit. Locate the area on a map and list some of the things of interest that you would like to see there. What would you pack for your trip?

HISTORY

PART 1:
How Russia Grew

Does history help to shape **culture**, or does culture make history? The answer may be a little of both.

Certainly, historical events like natural disasters, revolutions, and invasions by foreign armies affect the culture of a country. Russia has had plenty of these events in its long history.

In the ninth century, what is now known as the Commonwealth of Independent States (C.I.S.), was a vast **wilderness** with a small population. People grouped together in clans for safety and roamed the country searching for food and shelter. These people were called **nomads**. The clans were always on the move fighting each other and invading new territory. Each clan was ruled by a chief, the strongest and wisest man among its members.

In the ninth century, two Christian missionaries from the Byzantine Empire wanted to convert these clans to Christianity. In order to communicate with them, two Bulgarian monks, Cyril (SEER ril) and Methodius (meth O dee us), devised an alphabet for the clans' spoken language that was based on Greek letters. This alphabet was eventually called Cyrillic, and is the basis of the alphabet that the Russian language uses today.

The Rise and Fall of Kiev

The Russian state began in the ninth century with the development of the city of Kiev, near the Dnieper River, several hundred miles west of what is now Moscow. The ruler of Kiev was called "Grand Prince." This kingdom was only a tiny part of what is now the C.I.S.

Kievan society was made up of slaves and peasants, who worked the fields and lived on small farms, and elders, who governed under the direction of the grand prince. Kiev reached its peak of power in about A.D. 1055. At this time Russians shared a common culture and language. Many had adopted a form of Christianity. (In A.D. 988 Vladimir, the Grand Prince of Kiev, had converted to Eastern Orthodox Christianity. He made it the official religion and required his subjects to become Christians.) Yet Russia was not a nation in the same way as modern-day France or the United States. The country consisted of small villages and towns separated by wide distances, and a few larger cities, like Kiev and Novgorod. The towns were unsanitary, crowded, and dangerous. Laws were whatever the strongest chief said they were. There were no police around to protect people and there were no doctors. There was no guarantee that there would be food on the table the next day. Government consisted of the ruler and a few of his friends who usually came from the landowning class. These rich landowners were called **boyars**. Each city had an assembly called a "veche," in which all free adult males were allowed to vote.

R
E
V
I
E
W

Directions:
Number your paper from 1 to 5. Answer the following questions.
1. What are some factors that affect the culture of a country?
2. Describe Kievan society.
3. When was Kiev at the peak of its power?
4. How did two Christian missionaries change the history of the Russian people?
5. By what name were the rich landowners known?

PART 2:
The Mongols Invade

The Mongols (later known as Tatars) were a group of nomadic clans that lived in east-central Asia, between the great forests of Siberia and barren wastelands along the Chinese border. Their homeland was cold, **arid**, and mountainous. The Mongols were hunters, trappers, and fishers.

The Mongols began invading Russia in the early thirteenth century. In 1237, Batu, a grandson of the Mongol conqueror Genghis Khan, crossed the Volga River into Russia with an army of 200,000 Mongol warriors.

The Mongols captured town after town. If the inhabitants showed the slightest resistance, they were overcome and slaughtered. Kiev was one such victim. The Mongols stormed the city in 1240, destroyed it completely, and killed almost the entire population. The Mongols ruled Russia for the next 250 years.

This invasion is a good example of how history (in this case, the Mongol invasion) affects **culture**. The Mongol rule has had a powerful effect on Russian culture. Thousands of Mongol words found their way into the Russian language, where they remain today. The Russians also took on many of the Mongol ways of doing things. Many Russians accepted the Mongols' narrow view of government, which demanded absolute **obedience** to one man. During the Mongol conquest of Russia, which was roughly from the years 1237 to 1480, Western Europe was rapidly changing as new ideas and new ways of doing things grew. Under the Mongols, Russia was cut off from these new ideas and became suspicious of Western culture. This had a great effect on Russian growth and culture for hundreds of years.

Mongol warriors were expert camel riders as well as skilled horsemen. This photo shows a scene from "Time-Line," a PBS series that re-creates important events in the history of the world.

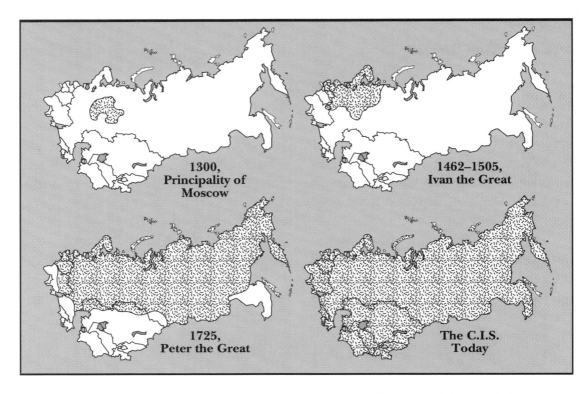

1300,
Principality of
Moscow

1462–1505,
Ivan the Great

1725,
Peter the Great

The C.I.S.
Today

Map Study: *This map shows Russia's territorial expansion from 1300 to today. When did the least amount of territorial expansion occur — before or after the time of Ivan the Great? When did the greatest amount of territorial expansion occur? Between 1300 and the time of Ivan the Great, did Russian territory expand more to the north or to the south?*

Moscow Is Founded

Moscow was founded in 1147 as a military outpost in a region called Muscovy. It was close to several rivers, which gave it access to the Volga River and the Caspian Sea.

Moscow gradually became the most powerful city in Russia. The city was built around a fort called the Kremlin. The Kremlin became the administrative and religious center of Russia. The Kremlin is still the center of power in Russia.

Under Grand Prince Ivan III, also called Ivan the Great, the state of Muscovy became the center of Russia. It grew rapidly by seizing and absorbing territory. This swift expansion laid the groundwork for the great country of **diverse** cultures and different peoples that Russia was to become. Ivan the Great ruled Muscovy from 1462 to 1505. In 1480, Ivan the Great refused to pay taxes to the Mongols, and Mongol **domination** of Russia ended.

Exciting things began to happen. Many foreigners, mostly Greeks and Italians, came to Moscow, bringing their knowledge and their books. Russia was becoming less backward, and the cultural mix of people and **customs** continued to grow.

Ivan the Terrible

Ivan IV, also known as Ivan the Terrible, became the ruler in 1547. He called himself "czar," or emperor. (Czar is now spelled **tsar**. The word comes from the Latin "Caesar.") Until 1560, Ivan did a good job. He made new laws that favored the people and improved trade and relations with European nations and with Turkey. Many think that Ivan then went insane. He began to mistreat his people. He died in 1584.

Ivan the Terrible was known to get rid of his enemies by torturing them first and then having them beheaded.

The "Time of Troubles"

For the next 30 years, Russia went through the "Time of Troubles"—a period of weak governments, **famine**, civil war, invasion, and mass confusion. It was not until 1613 that some order was restored and a new tsar was chosen from one of the great families of Moscow.

R
E
V
I
E
W

Directions:
Number your paper from 1 to 5. Answer the following questions.
1. In what year was the city of Moscow founded?
2. Why was Ivan IV known as "Ivan the Terrible"?
3. What were some of the exciting things that began to happen during the reign of Ivan the Great?
4. What effect did the Mongol invasion have on Russian culture?
5. Describe the homeland and lifestyle of the Mongols.

PART 3:
The Romanov Dynasty Begins

In 1613, Michael Romanov became tsar. The Romanov family ruled Russia for the next 300 years, until the Bolshevik Revolution in 1917.

Between the reigns of Peter I (Peter the Great, 1682-1725), and Catherine II (Catherine the Great, 1762-1796), Russia acquired much territory and greatly increased the cultural mix that marks the country today.

Peter the Great began building a new capital in 1703 on a swamp in northern Russia and named it St. Petersburg. He also brought industry and Western culture and ideas to Russia and founded the now famous Academy of Sciences in St. Petersburg in 1724. The education system was improved. Peter was called "Teacher of His People." Peter brought Russia into the modern age. He died in 1725.

Napoleon Invades Russia

When Alexander I became tsar in 1801, Russia was the largest country in the world and had great mineral wealth. Yet there were few good schools, and most citizens could not read or write. Although there was a small class of educated nobles, who lived on large estates, many millions of peasants lived in poverty and ignorance. Alexander I did away with the secret police who had been around since the time of Ivan the Terrible, and ordered a new code of justice.

All reforming activity ended in June of 1812 when Napoleon Bonaparte invaded Russia with an army of over

---

St. Petersburg

St. Petersburg is the second largest city in the Commonwealth of Independent States with a population of more than four million. Moscow is the largest city with a population of more than eight million.

St. Petersburg was built by Tsar Peter the Great in the early eighteenth century. It is an important shipping, commercial, cultural, and industrial center and is called Russia's "window to the West."

The name of the city was changed to Leningrad in the 1920s in honor of V. I. Lenin, the leader of the Communist movement in Russia. It was changed back to St. Petersburg after the fall of the Communist party.

The people of St. Petersburg are proud of their role in World War II, when the city was nearly surrounded by German armies and withstood a 900-day siege. A huge graveyard containing many of the victims of that siege is a national shrine.

Ironically, in the bitter winter of 1990, many people in Germany (along with many other nations) sent tons of food packages to the city to help feed its elderly citizens, many of whom had lost children in the war and had no one to look after them.

600,000 men. On September 7, 1812, the two armies fought the great Battle of Borodino. Many soldiers on both sides died, and the Russians withdrew toward Moscow.

The French entered Moscow on September 14, only to find that the Russians had burned it down to deny them shelter during the coming Russian winter. A month later, the French were almost out of food and Napoleon decided to retreat. The retreat soon turned into a rout, and the French began to run for their lives. Of the more than 600,000 troops of the Grand Army that had invaded Russia in June, about 400,000 died in battle or from starvation.

The Decembrists

Alexander I died suddenly on December 1, 1825, and Nicholas I became tsar of Russia. Almost at once, he had to deal with a revolt.

The Decembrists (so named because they revolted in the month of December) were young, patriotic officers in the Russian army. They formed a secret so-

This triumphal arch in Moscow's Kutuzov Avenue was built to mark Russia's victory over Napoleon.

ciety whose purpose was to reform the government, abolish serfdom, and establish freedom of speech and press.

The Decembrists revolted on December 25, 1825. Nicholas I sent troops to end their small uprising. Their action upset Nicholas because the Decembrists were educated members of the upper classes. The tsars depended on the upper classes to support the government. Their revolt occurred right at the center of power and was a major step leading to the Bolshevik Revolution of 1917.

R E V I E W

Directions:
Number your paper from 1 to 5. Answer the following questions.
1. What important changes did the Romanovs bring during their rule?
2. Why did Alexander I stop his reforming activity?
3. How did the Russians turn back the French from Moscow?
4. Name three things that Peter the Great did. Why were they important?
5. What were the goals of the Decembrists? Why was the revolt so important?

PART 4:
The Romanov Dynasty
Draws to a Close

Alexander II became tsar in 1855 at the age of 37. He was the first great **liberal** tsar. He immediately turned to the problem of the serfs. The serfs were, in effect, slaves. They owned almost nothing. They couldn't leave the farm where they worked or even marry without the approval of the landowner.

Tsar Alexander II abolished serfdom and improved education, the courts, and public health before a terrorist bomb took his life in 1881.

Alexander II Frees the Serfs

On March 3, 1861, a little more than a month before the American Civil War began over the issue of slavery, Alexander II signed an Emancipation Proclamation freeing the serfs. Although their situation was improved somewhat, the serfs still did not own the land outright and continued to be denied many personal freedoms. The Emancipation Proclamation was a case of too little, too late. Despite Alexander's reforms, terrorist groups began to form to overthrow the tsar and start over again with a different kind of government. In 1881, Alexander II was killed by a terrorist bomb in St. Petersburg.

The Last of the Tsars

Alexander III succeeded his father in 1881 and began changing things back to the way they were. Alexander III died in 1894. He was followed by his son, Nicholas II, the last tsar and one of the most tragic figures in history.

Nicholas II became tsar in 1894 at the age of 26. Although he may have been suitable as a college professor or shopkeeper, he was not able to rule a country of 130 million people that covered one-sixth of the world's land area. He believed in one-man rule and actually knew little about his own people and their problems. However, the Russian people at first loved Nicholas II and called him "Little Father."

Marxism and the Bolsheviks

There were many forces gathering that wanted to change Russia. One of these forces was Marxism. Karl Marx was a German **philosopher** and writer who urged the working class to revolt against its masters and take over the government. All property would then belong to the state.

Parties began to form to overthrow the Russian government. One of the parties was the Russian Social Democratic Labor party, also known as Bolsheviks (BOHL shuh viks), that eventually became the Communist party. A major party leader was V. I. Lenin, a Marxist.

People Lose Faith in the Tsar

In 1904, Russia went to war against Japan. Russian armies were defeated and a Russian fleet was sunk by the Japanese in a famous naval battle in the Straits of Tsushima.

The Russian people began to lose faith in the tsar. On Sunday, January 22, 1905, a huge crowd led by a priest, Father Gapon, marched on the tsar's palace in St. Petersburg. The crowd was bringing a petition to the tsar asking for more freedom. Cossack cavalry was waiting. The order was given to fire, and men, women, and children fell dead. Hundreds were killed. The world was shocked at the news of **Bloody Sunday.**

"Strike fever" took over Russia. Merchants closed their doors to business. Teachers wouldn't teach, cooks wouldn't cook, and doctors and lawyers closed their offices.

Nicholas II gave in. On October 30, 1905, he issued a famous public statement called the **October Manifesto**. In his **manifesto**, he guaranteed many freedoms unheard of in Russia. This event was so important that it is often called the Revolution of 1905.

R E V I E W

Directions:
Number your paper from 1 to 5. Answer the following questions.
1. What was the condition of the serfs when Alexander II freed them in 1861?
2. Name two things that led to the downfall of Tsar Nicholas II.
3. What did Karl Marx and his followers want their society to be like?
4. Describe the events of Bloody Sunday.
5. Why was the *October Manifesto* important to the Russian people?

PART 5:
War and Revolution

Europe was divided into an armed camp by the year 1914. Of the major powers, on one side were Russia, France, and Great Britain; on the other were Austria-Hungary, Germany, and Italy. (Italy would later change sides and fight against Germany and Austria. Turkey would then take Italy's place in the Triple Alliance.)

World War I Brings Disaster

War began through a series of complicated events that started after the **assassination** of Archduke Franz Ferdinand, who was to be the next king of Austria-Hungary. He and his wife were killed by a student revolutionary on June 28, 1914, in the city of Sarajevo in what was then Serbia (now Bosnia-Herzegovina).

Austria-Hungary used the assassination as an excuse to declare war on Serbia on July 28, 1914. After a series of declarations of war, World War I began in earnest. Russian armies invaded East Prussia, a part of Germany, with the intent of capturing Berlin, the German capital. The Germans defeated the Russians in the battles of Tannenberg in August and Mazurian Lakes in September of 1914.

Romanov Rule Comes to an End

By 1917, things began to fall apart on the Russian home front. Because there were so many men in the army few people were left to work on the farms and in the factories. Food shortages began to appear. By March 10, the entire capital city of Petrograd (now St. Petersburg) was full of soldiers, police, and wild mobs. Before the day of March 12, 1917 was over, mobs were in control of most government buildings. Advisers to Tsar Nicholas told him he should **abdicate** from the Russian throne. He did so on March 16, 1917, suddenly ending the 300-year-old Romanov rule.

The Provisional Government

A Provisional Government was formed by various government officials. The Provisional Government was later led by lawyer Alexander Kerensky. In Petrograd, the revolutionary workers formed their own kind of government through **soviets** (councils).

The Provisional Government might have been successful in ordinary times, but these were not ordinary times. The new government had to deal with a country at war, food shortages, an empty treasury, and a violent population that wanted change. It declared that it would continue the war against Germany. The people, however, were tired of the war.

Into the middle of this disaster stepped V. I. Lenin and Leon Trotsky, two Bolshevik leaders. Lenin had returned from **exile** in mid-April of 1917. He immediately called for an end to the war.

By the middle of 1917, the Russian army had collapsed, and army and navy units within Russia revolted. Lenin and Trotsky planned a Bolshevik takeover. On November 7, 1917 (October 25 on the old Russian calendar), armed workers took over important points in Petrograd.

The cruiser Aurora *fired the shot that signaled the rebel charge to the Winter Palace and the beginning of the Bolshevik Revolution. Today,* Aurora *is a national shrine and is permanently docked on the Neva River in St. Petersburg, not far from the Winter Palace.*

The Bolsheviks Take Over

A few days later, Moscow was taken over by the Bolsheviks. The Provisional Government was through after only a few months in existence and the Bolsheviks were in power. Lenin was determined to make peace with the Germans and declared an **armistice** in December of 1917.

Russian and German representatives met at Brest-Litovsk in Poland and signed a peace treaty on March 3, 1918. Later that same year, Lenin moved the Russian capital from Petrograd to Moscow because of Moscow's more central location. Lenin by then had abolished all private property. All land, industry, and natural wealth became the property of the state. By 1922, the Bolsheviks had become the Communist party, and Russia had become the Union of Soviet Socialist Republics.

HISTORY

R E V I E W

Directions:
Number your paper from 1 to 5. Answer the following questions.
1. How were the major powers divided during World War I?
2. What caused the end of Romanov rule?
3. What two governments were trying to run Russia at the same time?
4. Name three things that Lenin did once the Bolsheviks were in power.
5. Why do you think the Provisional Government failed?

PART 6:
Stalin, the Five-Year Plan, and World War II

Lenin still had several problems. Many people in his own country were opposed to communism. The result was civil war in Russia.

The Russian Civil War was destructive and confusing. The sides were divided into the Whites and the Reds. The Whites wanted to overthrow Lenin and the Communists (the Reds). The Reds eventually won a war that lasted two bloody years.

Stalin Becomes Dictator

Lenin was considered the founder of the Soviet Union. By the 1920s, he had tightened his control of the country. When he died in January of 1924, a power struggle developed between Leon Trotsky and Joseph Stalin. Trotsky was the Communist party's leading thinker, while Stalin was its chief administrator. When Lenin died, Stalin was ready to take over. Because he was the general secretary of the Communist party, he was able to give many people jobs. This helped him in his struggle with Trotsky.

The Five-Year Plan

By 1929, Stalin was dictator of the Soviet Union. He proposed the first of his famous five-year plans to guide the Soviet Union to economic health. The plan had two major goals: the increase of heavy industry and the combination of small peasant farms into **collectives**, or huge farms owned by the state. It was his farm policy that caused the most suffering.

The peasants did not want to give up their land. They resisted by killing **livestock** and destroying crops. Stalin sent troops into the villages and burned them down. Millions of people were sent to prison labor camps in Siberia.

The Great Purge

In the mid-1930s, Stalin began a public program of terror called the **Great Purge.** The terror began in late 1934, when one of Stalin's trusted helpers was assassinated. Stalin used this as an excuse to bring several people to trial for the murder. Thousands of Communist party members were arrested. Some were given fake trials, then shot or sent to Siberia. Most prisoners sent to Siberia never returned.

World War II

While Stalin was ridding Russia of his enemies, World War II was rapidly approaching. Adolf Hitler, dictator of Germany and head of the Nazi party, had rearmed Germany after its defeat in World War I. On September 1, 1939, Germany invaded Poland from one side. A few days later, the Soviet Union invaded Poland from the other side. Stalin and Hitler had a secret agreement to divide up Polish lands between them. France and Great Britain were honor-bound by treaty to defend Poland. By September 3, both countries had declared war on Germany. Poland fought bravely, but in less than three weeks it no longer existed.

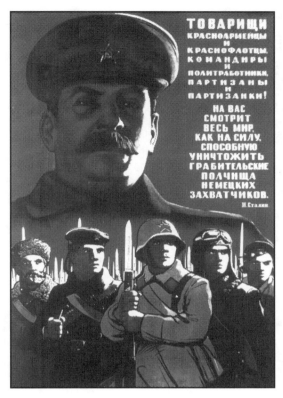

Joseph Stalin is pictured on this Soviet World War II poster that informs Russians that the world looks on them as "the force that can exterminate the predatory hordes of German invaders."

Stalin took over the three small countries of Lithuania, Estonia, and Latvia on the Baltic Sea in 1940 and made them part of the Soviet Union. A year and a half later, on June 22, 1941, Hitler sent two million soldiers and thousands of tanks and planes through the part of Poland occupied by the Soviet Union and into Russia itself. By mid-July of 1941,

SPOTLIGHT
S T O R Y

The Battle of Stalingrad

The Battle of Stalingrad during World War II was the turning point in the war between Germany and the Soviet Union. Until then, the war was going Germany's way. After Stalingrad, the Russians took the offensive and drove the Germans all the way back to Berlin and final defeat.

At the time of the battle, Stalingrad was a city of about 500,000 people. It had a lot of heavy war industry. The city was important because nothing could go up or down the Volga River without passing it. In other words, the city of Stalingrad controlled this major trade route.

The Soviets dedicated this monument to their World War II victory at Stalingrad. At the top of the monument stands a huge statue of a woman holding a sword, symbolizing the defense of the city against any future invaders.

The Germans reached Stalingrad in August of 1942. The Russians resisted stubbornly and fought for every house in the city. Most of the buildings were destroyed. Thousands of soldiers on both sides died in the rubble.

In January of 1943, a huge Soviet army suddenly attacked through bitter cold and blinding snow. The German Sixth Army was surrounded. Hitler ordered its leader, General Paulus, to fight to the last man rather than surrender. Hitler also sent an army to try to break through to the Sixth Army, but it was not successful.

With his army running out of food and ammunition, General Paulus decided to surrender rather than continue to fight against hopeless odds. More than 300,000 German troops were killed or captured during the battle. Of the 91,000 prisoners taken at Stalingrad, fewer than 5,000 returned to Germany after the war.

Stop and Review
Write the answers to these questions on your paper.
1. Why was the Battle of Stalingrad a turning point in the war between Germany and the Soviet Union?
2. On what river is Stalingrad located?
3. What is the importance of the city's location?
4. What did Hitler order General Paulus to do at Stalingrad?
5. Out of the 91,000 German soldiers taken prisoner at Stalingrad, how many returned to Germany after the war?

the Germans had driven deep inside Russia. In mid-August, the Germans attacked the Ukraine and captured the city of Kiev, the heart of ancient Russia. A German army moved toward Moscow, the Soviet capital. The Germans got within sight of Moscow before being pushed back in bloody fighting.

An abandoned horse searches for food amidst the rubble of Stalingrad (now Volgograd), December 1942.

A Turning Point in the War

In the summer of 1942, the Germans marched on Stalingrad (now Volgograd), a large industrial city on the Volga River. The Russians and Germans fought for months in and around the city. The German army was surrounded and destroyed in early 1943. It was the turning point in the war.

After Stalingrad, the Russians took the offensive, and by 1944 the Germans were in full retreat. Also, in June of 1944, Great Britain and the United States invaded France and began a drive from the west against Germany. With the Allies driving from the west and the Russians from the east, the German armies began to cave in. The Russians surrounded Berlin, the German capital, on April 25, 1945, and captured it on May 2. Five days later, the Germans surrendered. Hitler had committed suicide on April 30.

World War II had left Russia in ruins. Russians dead from the fighting, disease, and hunger were said to number 20 million. One out of every ten Russians had died. More than 1,700 cities and 70,000 villages were in ruins. Leningrad, for example, had been surrounded by the Germans for 900 days. During this time, many citizens of Leningrad had starved to death.

HISTORY

R E V I E W

Directions:
Number your paper from 1 to 5. Answer the following questions.
1. Describe Stalin's first Five-Year Plan and its effect on the Soviet people.
2. What was the Great Purge?
3. Why was the Battle of Stalingrad so important?
4. Why did France and Great Britain come to the aid of Poland?
5. What position did Stalin hold in the Communist party? Why did this position give him so much power?

PART 7:
The Cold War

The Soviet Union was now one of the two great powers in the world. The United States was the other one. Communist governments took over in Eastern Europe in the countries of Poland, Czechoslovakia, Romania, Hungary, Bulgaria, Albania, East Germany, and Yugoslavia.

The Two Superpowers

The United States and the Soviet Union, the two **superpowers**, did not get along. This led to what was called the **cold war**. The two countries didn't trust each other and disagreed about many things. However, they never actually had a shooting war.

The contest between the United States and the Soviet Union revealed itself in defeated Germany. The two coun-

tries argued over how to handle Germany. In 1949, the West German Federal Republic was created, with the city of Bonn as its capital. A peoples' republic of East Germany was created and controlled by the Communist party.

In 1961, East Germany built a wall between East and West Berlin to keep people in the east from escaping to West Berlin. (In November of 1989, the East German leadership, in a dramatic response to the demands of its people, granted free **access** to West Berlin through the Berlin Wall, which began to come down.)

Joseph Stalin Dies

Joseph Stalin's death was announced on March 5, 1953. The leadership picture now became confused as several people jockeyed for position to succeed Stalin. Nikita Khrushchev, (krush CHAWF) a favorite of Stalin's who had come up through the party ranks, proved to be the strongest challenger. He became the Soviet leader in 1954.

The colorful Nikita Khrushchev traveled the country to sell himself to the people. In 1956, he exposed Stalin as a murderer in a speech to the Communist party Congress. Khrushchev's policies were far different from Stalin's. The labor camps were allowed to empty. There was even some freedom of discussion allowed in the Soviet Union.

Relations between the Soviet Union and the United States were crucial to world peace. Khrushchev said that war between the two countries did not have to happen. His policy was called **peaceful coexistence**. This meant that the two countries could avoid war but still compete against each other.

The closest the Soviet Union and the United States came to war was in October of 1962 in what became known as the Cuban missile crisis. The United States learned that the Soviet Union had missile bases on the island of Cuba, just 90 miles from American shores. President John F. Kennedy ordered a blockade of Cuba to prevent more missiles from reaching Cuba. The world watched tensely for days as Russian ships carrying missiles approached Cuba. Would they turn back in the face of the United States Navy? They did, and the Russians agreed to Kennedy's terms.

Although Khrushchev improved relations with Western nations, many of his policies at home were not as successful. His farm program was a failure. In 1962 and 1963, the Soviet Union had to buy large amounts of wheat from the United States and Canada. In 1964, Khrushchev was thrown out of office and forced to retire from public life.

The Brezhnev Years

After Khrushchev left office in October of 1964, Leonid Brezhnev (BREHZH nehf) and Aleksey Kosygin (kuh SEE guhn) rose to control the country. A long but quiet struggle for power resulted. By 1971, Brezhnev, as head of the Communist party, was the more important of the two.

Brezhnev tried to ease the tension between the Soviet Union and the Western countries. Trade between East and West increased. The United States and the Soviet Union also began talks to decrease the number of nuclear weapons on both sides. In 1972, they agreed to limit such weapons. Within the Soviet Union, people began to demand more freedom.

HISTORY

Afghanistan Invaded

In December of 1979, the Soviet Union invaded Afghanistan, a small mountainous country on the Soviet Union's south-central border. Afghanistan had a Communist government, but that government was tottering. Afghan rebels fought back bitterly. It was ten years before Soviet armies were withdrawn.

Many foreign countries were angry at the Soviet invasion. U.S. President Jimmy Carter limited wheat shipments to the Soviet Union. He also refused to allow American athletes to participate in the 1980 Summer Olympic Games, which were held in Moscow.

Meanwhile, there was trouble in Poland. Strikes and unrest by Polish labor unions under the name **Solidarity**

Soviet troops in Kabul, Afghanistan, in January of 1980.

The Varangians

The name "Russia" is believed to be derived from the ancient Varangian word, "rus," meaning "ruddy" or "fair-skinned" men.

The Varangians were powerful Viking warriors from what are now Finland and Norway. Some historians think that it was the Varangians who laid the foundations for the city of Kiev, the center of ancient Russia; others think it was the Slavs.

---

plagued the ruling Communist government. Finally, in 1989, Poland was allowed to hold its first free elections under Communist rule. Poland was the first Communist country ever to hold free elections.

Mikhail Gorbachev Teaches the World Two Russian Words

In March of 1985, Mikhail Gorbachev, at age 54, became head of the Communist party and leader of the Soviet Union. There was unrest throughout the country. Parts of the Soviet Union wanted more control over their own affairs. Some areas like Estonia, a small Baltic country that had been taken over after World War II, even wanted complete freedom from the Soviet Union. Gorbachev recognized all of these problems. In response, he made two Russian words famous throughout the world.

The words are **perestroika** and

glasnost. *Perestroika* means "restructuring." In simple terms, Gorbachev meant to change the Soviet economy so that it would work more efficiently. He also called for greater political power for government bodies elected by the people. In March of 1989, the Soviet Union held its first free but limited elections. Many candidates opposed to the old Communist ways of doing things were swept into power.

Glasnost means "openness." For most of its history, Russia had been a closed society. Its leaders didn't tell its own people or the rest of the world what was going on. Even the greatest disasters, like floods or earthquakes, were kept as secret as possible. No foreigners could travel anywhere in the Soviet Union without permission.

Gorbachev said that the Soviet Union would now deal openly and honestly with everyone, even its own people, and that Russians could speak out against the government without fear of going to prison.

In February of 1990, the **Central Committee** of the Communist party

A peace dove sits on the head of former Soviet President Mikhail Gorbachev as he sets another bird free during a trip on the Sea of Galilee in Israel.

voted to allow a multi-party system in the Soviet Union. After 73 years of one-party control, many Western observers believed that the country was now moving toward a more representative form of government and that the Communist party might lose some of its political power.

HISTORY

R
E
V
I
E
W

Directions:
Number your paper from 1 to 5. Answer the following questions.
1. Define the term *cold war* and give an example of it.
2. What was the Cuban missile crisis?
3. How did the limited free elections in March of 1989 affect the Communist party in the Soviet Union?
4. Why was the relationship between the Soviet Union and the United States important to world peace?
5. What problems or risks, if any, do you think the Soviet government took with Gorbachev's policy of glasnost and perestroika?

PART 8:
The Rise of Boris Yeltsin

Mikhail Gorbachev was on the right track, but he didn't go fast enough or far enough toward total democracy to stave off the stunning events that were to develop in 1991. Two factors contributed to his eventual downfall. One was his unsuccessful attempt to tread a line between the Communist party, which wanted to preserve the Soviet Union under the old rules, and the new **radicals** of Russian politics, who wanted total democracy.

Russian President Boris Yeltsin and Mikhail Gorbachev, president of the Congress of People's Deputies, discuss a new constitution.

The other was the rise of one of the remarkable figures of modern Russian history—Boris Nikolayevich Yeltsin. Yeltsin and Gorbachev were born in the same year—1931—one month apart.

Yeltsin was born to peasant parents in a log cabin near Sverdlovsk, now Yekaterinburg, in the Ural Mountains. He tells the story of how he was nearly drowned in the baptismal tub by a drunken Orthodox priest who forgot to lift his head out of the water. He was rescued by his screaming mother.

The priest was not particularly worried. "Well, if he can survive such an ordeal it means he's a good tough lad. I name him Boris." There were many ordeals to follow.

Yeltsin's birth came in the middle of Stalin's farm collectivization program in which crops were taken from the peasants, who were then often left to starve in their huts. "We lived in a small hut with one cow," Yeltsin later wrote. "We had a horse, but it died so we had nothing to plough with." Then the cow died and Yeltsin's father went to a **collective** farm to work. The Yeltsins—grandfather, parents, and three small children—slept on the floor, huddling together with the family goat to keep warm.

Poor Background

Gorbachev also came from a poor background, but there was one major difference. Gorbachev was a third-generation Communist party member. Yeltsin's family had no Communist links. Gorbachev was faithful to communist ideals. Yeltsin went along with the Communists because there was no choice in the Russia of his youth.

Yeltsin actually had no interest in politics while growing up. His interest

Mikhail Gorbachev

Despite his loss of power and popularity in his homeland, former Soviet President Mikhail Gorbachev stands as one of the great political leaders of the twentieth century.

Between 1985 and 1990, Gorbachev freed Eastern Europe from Communist domination. He permitted the destruction of the Berlin Wall and German reunification. He signed the first agreements for nuclear arms reductions and the withdrawal of Soviet armed forces from Europe. For these, he won the Nobel Peace Prize.

At home, he broke the power monopoly of the Communist party and opened the door to political dissent and a multi-party system. He brought freedom of speech and press to the Soviet Union, insisted on free elections and a legislature free of domination by the Communist party, and encouraged the growth of new, younger leaders.

Most important, he introduced the idea that society should be ruled by law and not by the whim of a Communist party leader.

He was caught between the conservatives of the Communist party and the radicals, who wanted total democracy. He tried to please both sides, and he tried to do too much too fast, but he will go down in history as a great world leader.

was in sports—volleyball especially. He played and coached volleyball and ran the college sports association at Urals Polytechnical Institute. After graduating in 1955, he decided to go into civil engineering and was soon laying bricks at a construction site. He advanced to chief engineer for his district and acquired a reputation as a man who could get things done. In the early 1960s, he joined the Communist party because this was the only path to success. His rise was rapid after that. He became a full-time Communist official responsible for all construction in Sverdlovsk province. In 1976, he became Sverdlovsk's Communist party first secretary, an important job. It meant that Leonid Brezhnev, then leader of the Soviet Union, recognized Yeltsin's abilities. Yeltsin gained a reputation of being one of the few leaders unafraid of meeting the people and trying to settle their grievances.

In April 1985, a few weeks after Gorbachev's appointment as general secretary of the Communist party, which in effect made him ruler of the Soviet Union, Yeltsin went to Moscow as supervisor of construction for the entire Soviet Union. A few months later he became head of the Communist party in Moscow. He was now near the top level of the party. And it was here that Yeltsin developed the style that was to make him a hero of the people. Within days of his appointment, Yeltsin was touring downtown shops, waiting in line for buses, and catching the metro, all unheard of for **pampered** Communist officials.

He also cleaned out many of the incompetent old-line Communists from important positions. Then came the biggest promotion. In 1986 he was appointed a candidate to the **Politburo**, the Communist party's most important policy-making body. Soon after, he stepped out of line. He made a speech in which he criticized special privileges for Communist leaders. This was hitting at the most vital part of Communist control at all levels. The party bound its members by special benefits. The lowest rank might receive a monthly package of food, **zakaz** (order), with some scarce sausage or a couple tins of crab meat. Then it might be access to a car pool, or his own chauffeur-driven car and a roomy apartment as the official moved up the party ladder. Soon, the official would do anything to keep his privileges, and he would fight anyone who attacked those privileges.

A Famous Feud

Yeltsin attacked privilege and Gorbachev defended it. Yeltsin won the support of the people for his stand,

Gorbachev the support of Communist party members. It was the beginning of a famous and fateful feud between two strong men. The fate of the Soviet Union, an empire built over a thousand years, hinged on the outcome.

Ukrainian women shout while waving their coupons to buy butter at a state-owned shop in Kiev. Despite their economic situation, Ukrainians are rejoicing over their independence.

The Communist party reacted to Yeltsin's charges of privilege and incompetence with scorn and anger. "Khrushchev tried to make us dress like peasants, but he didn't succeed and neither will you," one member said. Another sent him a note that said: "We've always stolen, and we'll go on stealing. Go back to Sverdlovsk while there is still time."

According to John Morrison, in his book *Boris Yeltsin: From Bolshevik to Democrat*, Yeltsin began to realize that the Communist party was against reform and change of any kind, and was in fact the main obstacle to reform. In late 1987, Yeltsin was under great pressure from party regulars to keep his mouth shut. Yeltsin realized he was making no headway to end corruption and incompetence. In October, he resigned as a candidate for the Politburo. He also quit as party chief of Moscow. These acts were unheard of in the political leadership of the Soviet Union. Yeltsin was voluntarily giving up his **dacha**, with its marble floors, the cooks, the gardeners, and the big, black limousine. He was breaking the golden chains that were supposed to hold him. The party viciously attacked him and said that he had disgraced himself. It was his lowest point. Yeltsin had moved too quickly against the party and paid the price, but the public was disturbed by the course of events. Gorbachev declared that Yeltsin's political life was ended, but the public didn't agree. Yeltsin was the most popular man in the Soviet Union. Gorbachev was popular in other countries, but he was rapidly losing favor at home.

Yeltsin's Return

Meanwhile, the reforms that Gorbachev had set in motion began to get out of control. New times were on the way. On March 26, 1989, the Soviet Union held its first nation-wide elections since 1917 to elect members to the **Congress of People's Deputies**, the Soviet ruling body. Yeltsin stood for election and won Moscow's at-large seat easily. Of the 6.8 million registered voters, 5.1 million voted for Yeltsin. He had come back from the politically dead and was on his way despite bitter opposition from the Communist party, which still held the balance of power in the Soviet Union. The election was Gorbachev's idea. He wanted to keep the conservatives under control, but he had set in motion forces that he couldn't control. It was a turning point in Soviet history.

As a member of the Congress, Yeltsin called for land reform, press freedom, and a law restricting the power of the Communist party. Yeltsin, huge physically, was like a great Russian bear, flailing at all the failures of the government under Gorbachev and the Communist party. Thirty years earlier, he would have been shot or imprisoned for his words, but those days had long since passed. One American writer described Yeltsin in this way: "He was like a bear on a skateboard. He never once fell off, but it was close."

Gorbachev Fights for Control

Meanwhile, Soviet politics was in turmoil as the military, the KGB (the So-

Soviet President Mikhail Gorbachev points to a copy of his proposal to abolish the centrally controlled state of the Soviet Union.

viet security force), and Communist party leaders began to understand the danger they were in. If democracy came to the U.S.S.R., they would lose their power and privileges. And democracy was coming. In February 1990, the Communist party gave up its monopoly on political power, in effect paving the way for a multi-party system like that of the Western powers. The Communist party was dead but didn't quite know it.

A woman reads the "Kuranty" or Tower Clock newspaper on Moscow's subway. The front page carries the story of former Soviet President Mikhail Gorbachev's resignation.

Events began to move rapidly. Gorbachev told the Congress of People's Deputies that he needed a stronger position in order to keep the Soviet Union from coming apart. On March 13, 1990, he was voted into the Soviet presidency by the Congress and given greater powers to run the country. Unfortunately, the "nationalities problem" that Gorbachev so badly misunderstood began to shake the Soviet Union apart. If all the republics decided to leave the Soviet Union, Gorbachev would be a man without a government to run.

It was his aim to keep the country together by any means. It was Yeltsin's aim to eventually make Russia a democratic, independent country whose laws would take precedence over those of the Soviet Union. Yeltsin moved into a position to make his dream come true when he was elected chairman of the **Supreme Soviet**, the standing parliament of Russia and the body which would make the rules. In effect, Yeltsin was now running Russia, the largest and most influential republic in the Soviet Union by far. In June of 1991 he was elected president of Russia with strong powers delegated to him to lead the country. Yeltsin was the first national leader to be elected by the people in the thousand-year history of Russia. He won by a large margin despite the bitter opposition of the Communist party.

The last dramatic act in the Yeltsin-Gorbachev feud was about to begin.

The Communists Fight Back

Dark forces were gathering to destroy democracy. Before dawn on August 19, 1991, a black limousine drew up in front of the Moscow headquarters of the Tass news agency, the official voice of the Soviet government. A representative of the "U.S.S.R. State Committee on the State of the Emergency" left the limousine and went into Tass headquarters to announce that the Gorbachev era was over and the committee would take over the government.

This mysterious and previously unknown committee was made up of eight Communist office holders. The committee announced that Gorbachev was ill and was "unable to perform his duties." The truth was, Gorbachev was on vacation on the Black Sea. He discovered there was trouble when he tried to make a phone call to Moscow and found that the phone lines had been cut. Then he was confronted in his dacha by several of the plotters and asked to step down as Soviet leader. Gorbachev refused and was then put under house arrest.

Meanwhile, Boris Yeltsin was at his desk in the parliament building in Mos-

cow early on the morning of August 19. The streets of Moscow were choked with troops and tanks. Angry civilians, just becoming aware of what was happening, were shaking their fists and shouting at the soldiers to go away.

Resistance to the takeover was spotty. Many foreign leaders, as well as Soviet government officials, sat on the fence waiting to see which side would win. Then came the dramatic and courageous turning point. At mid-morning of August 19, Yeltsin marched out of his office and climbed aboard an army tank, where he read a proclamation denouncing the attempted takeover.

Yeltsin Risks His Life

"Soldiers, officers and generals, the clouds of terror and dictatorship are gathering over the whole country," he declared. "They must not be allowed to bring eternal night!" British Prime Minister John Majors called it a "moment of raw courage." Yeltsin placed his life on the line in the face of the tanks. The people of Moscow supported him. They came by the hundreds, then by the thousands, then by the hundreds of thousands to stand between Yeltsin and the army's guns. In three days the attempted takeover had collapsed because army troops refused to fire on their own people. The tank commanders turned their guns away from Yeltsin and his protectors while women paraded in front of the tanks with a huge banner that read, "Soldiers! Don't Shoot Your Mothers!"

The conspirators were arrested while attempting to flee the country. One killed himself. (The accused have had the charges against them reduced from treason to conspiracy to seize power.) They could face 8 to 15 years in prison.

Three civilians were killed when Russian soldiers in armored personnel carriers tried to clear a barricade. Two were shot in the head. One fell off a tank and was run over by it. The plotters had planned to send a special KGB force to storm Yeltsin's building, arrest or kill him and his assistants, and kill anyone else who got in the way. The special force decided at the last moment not to follow orders because of the huge crowd that protected Yeltsin.

Gorbachev was freed and hurried back to Moscow, but he came back to a suddenly different world. The changes he had begun in 1985 had made it impossible to turn the clock back to the days of harsh rule. Statues of former Bolshevik heroes were being toppled all over the country, and despite Gorbachev's stand against the people who tried to take over the government, he was no longer in favor with the people. Yeltsin

Finances, Disarmament

The United States and other Western powers, anxious to help the shaky democratic movement survive in Russia, have underwritten loans of up to $24 billion for that country. More help was expected as Russia's needs surfaced.

The Western countries and Russia have also speeded up the disarmament process. Thousands of tanks and guns are being destroyed, as well as hundreds of nuclear missiles. A major problem is the disposal of thousands of tons of deadly nerve gas, which are kept in storage tanks mostly in the U.S. and Russia.

Another major problem for Russia is the Black Sea fleet. Russia and the Ukraine have both claimed the 300-ship fleet. In August 1992 the two republics agreed to delay until 1995 division of the powerful but expensive fleet.

was the hero and Gorbachev's days were numbered.

On August 29, the Supreme Soviet voted to suspend all activities of the Communist party. The party in effect was dead. The Communist leaders who had attempted to take over the Soviet government and turn back the clock to the days of repression had achieved exactly the opposite. They had speeded up the rush to total democracy and the breakup of the Soviet Union.

More stunning events followed rapidly. Gorbachev resigned as general

Russian President Boris Yeltsin, left, is greeted by German Finance Minister Theo Waigel, right, as he arrives in Munich for a meeting with European leaders.

The End Is Near

It was just a matter of tying up the loose ends. On December 19, Russian President Boris Yeltsin ordered the seizure of the Kremlin and ordered functions of the Soviet government to be replaced by Russia. The unofficial end of the Soviet Union came on December 21 when 11 of the 15 republics signed agreements to create the Commonwealth of Independent States. The Baltic states and Georgia refused to join. (See box on the

secretary of the Communist party and accused the party of backing the attempted takeover. On September 6, 1991, he recognized the independence of the Baltic states: Estonia, Latvia, and Lithuania. The Ukraine, the third largest republic in the Soviet Union, in reality put an end to the Soviet Union by declaring its independence on September 8. Within a few days, Moldova, Azerbaijan, Kyrgyzstan, Uzbekistan, Georgia, Armenia, and Tajikistan followed. Gorbachev was suddenly a man without a country.

main elements of the C.I.S. agreement, on page 103.).

On December 25, 1992, Gorbachev announced his resignation from the presidency of the now non-existent Soviet Union, and the white, blue, and red flag of tsarist Russia was raised over the Kremlin, replacing the famous hammer and sickle flag of the Soviet Union.

Russian president Yeltsin had finally pushed aside Gorbachev and now assumed the leading role in the region. Gorbachev was hailed for starting in motion the events that finally freed Russia and the other republics from

Communist rule. He was regarded as a "great man" who had failed because he was too indecisive to cope with the radical changes that had come.

Yeltsin's—and Russia's—troubles were far from over. They had only begun. Rising prices, the shortage of food and goods, and the general disarray of Russian social and government structures brought about by the rapid changes made even Yeltsin's rule a shaky one as 1992 neared its end.

The first anniversary of the attempted coup was celebrated in August 1992, with four days of events, which included parades, concerts, and memorials. Yet despite the festivities, the mood among the population in general—even those who had defended the White House in Moscow—was subdued.

For many, the euphoria of throwing off Communist domination disappeared as they were battered by the effects of "shock-therapy" reforms. Many Russians expressed frustration over the past year's developments, saying the hardships caused by economic reform may cause people to give up on a **market** system. The leadership, they also complained, had not made needed political reforms, such as adopting a new constitution.

R E V I E W

Directions:
Number your paper from 1 to 4. Answer the following questions.
1. What two factors led to Gorbachev's downfall?
2. What was Boris Yeltsin's special interest while he was growing up?
3. What did the Communists fear they would lose if democracy came to Russia?
4. How did Yeltsin risk his life?

MAP SKILLS

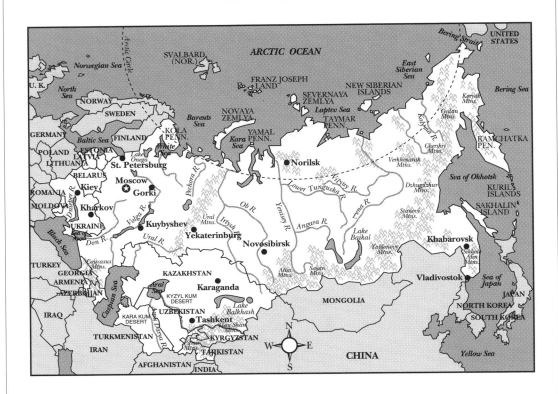

PHYSICAL FEATURES OF THE C.I.S.

Directions:

Number your paper from 1 to 11. Use the map on this page to help you answer the following questions.

1. Gorki is located on what river?
2. What river flows from the Ural Mountains into the Caspian Sea?
3. List three countries that border the C.I.S. to the south.
4. What country would you enter if you traveled directly south from Lake Baikal?
5. What ocean is north of the C.I.S.?
6. Name a city in the C.I.S. located north of the Arctic Circle.
7. What kind of land lies between the Caspian Sea and the Amu Darya River?
8. What sea would you cross traveling from the city of St. Petersburg to the coast of Sweden?
9. What mountains are closest to the Sea of Japan?
10. The United States (Alaska) and the C.I.S. are separated by what body of water?
11. What city is located near the Pamir Mountains?

CHAPTER 2 REVIEW

Summary of History

The Russian state began in the ninth century with the formation of the city of Kiev in what is now known as the Republic of Ukraine. The Mongol invasion of Russia in the thirteenth century destroyed Kiev and led to the rise of Moscow as a major center of the Russian state and culture.

The Russian state grew rapidly, first under the grand princes and then under the tsars, until its borders stretched 6,000 miles from Poland on the west to the Pacific Ocean in the east. The tsars ruled Russia until 1917. Nicholas II was forced to abdicate and the Bolshevik Revolution made the Communists rulers of the Soviet Union.

The Soviet Union fought Germany in World War II, and was later isolated from the rest of the world by the dictator Joseph Stalin. Mikhail Gorbachev became the Soviet leader in 1985 and tried to reform Communist society, but the democratic movement took control as a new leader, Boris Yeltsin, appeared. The Communist party was outlawed when some of its leaders tried to take over.

The Soviet Union broke into separate republics in December 1991, and the Commonwealth of Independent States came into being. Russia, with Yeltsin as president, was the dominant force in the new union.

Critical Thinking Skills

Directions: Give some serious thought to the questions below. Be sure to answer in complete sentences.

1. Do you think President Kennedy did the right thing in blocking Soviet ships from Cuba, even though a world war might have resulted? Explain.
2. Why was there still discontent after Alexander II freed the serfs?
3. Compare the leadership of Gorbachev and Yeltsin and explain why one failed and the other didn't.

4. Why did the Communists fail in their attempt to take over the Soviet government?

For Discussion

Directions: Discuss these questions with your class. Appoint one class member to write the ideas you discover on the board.

1. List some of the problems Russia faces under democracy. Discuss how you would solve them.
2. The Berlin Wall went up practically overnight and separated friends and family for years. Imagine you were a Berliner at the time. How would you have reacted if you had seen this barrier separating you and your best friend?
3. The Communists attempted to take over the Soviet government in August 1991. What would you have done when you found out about the attempt?

Write It!

Directions: A timeline is a way of showing when events occur in relation to one another. The timeline can be vertical (up and down) or horizontal (left to right). Prepare a timeline listing events discussed in this chapter. Be sure to list events in their correct order and include dates if they are given.

For You to Do

Directions: As a class, make up separate cards about people, places, and events that were discussed in this chapter. Each card should list a few facts about the person or event named on that card. Shuffle the cards and have them distributed to class members. Divide the class into teams and play "20 Questions."

THE FORMER SOVIET REPUBLICS

Chapter 3

- Athletes from the former Soviet Union participated in the 1992 Olympic Games as the Unified Team.
- The names of many cities, towns, and republics have been changed since the breakup of the Soviet Union.
- Statues of former Communist heroes have come tumbling down in the former Soviet Union and other former Communist states.
- Severe damage to the **environment** is one of the major legacies of Communist rule.

PART 1:
What Nationality Are You?

What is a nationality, or **ethnic**, group? It is a group of people who are united by a common background, **tradition**, language, and **customs**. These things have developed over many hundreds of years.

Until December 1991, the Soviet Union was a huge country that included many ethnic groups. This was one of the reasons the country broke up and part of the former Soviet Union became the Commonwealth of Independent States. Each ethnic group wanted its complete independence. But even within the new arrangement there are divisions of ethnic groups, and these divisions continue to cause trouble.

Thousands of years ago, tribal groups

roamed what became the C.I.S. in search of food and security, much as certain groups of Native Americans roamed what is now the United States. Eventually, these groups settled in areas that suited them best. They established a **culture** that was different from those of other tribes. Each tribe had a language and customs that were different from those of its neighbors.

So why aren't the 50 states of the United States organized along ethnic lines, while the republics of the former Soviet Union were? It is because the two developed differently.

The Different Paths

In America, the coming of the Europeans swept aside the separate native groups. Eventually, the Native Americans were driven from their homelands and sent to reservations where many still live today. Early settlement of what is now the eastern United States was mostly English, and the English became the **predominant** ethnic group in early America.

In Russia, the tribal groups mostly stayed in place and were absorbed into the country as it grew. There were invasions and **infiltration** by other nationality groups, but these ethnic, or tribal, groups generally kept their identities and went on with their ways. Today, many of these groups strive to keep their identities. To understand nationality, or ethnic, groups in what is now the Commonwealth of Independent States, think about the nationality groups that make up the United States.

A majority of the first settlers in what is now the United States came from England. Since then, there have been waves of **immigrants** from many countries. Most of them were escaping from poverty to find a better way of life. Included in this vast migration from the continent of Europe were the Germans, Irish, Italians, Greeks, Poles, and Jews. These immigrants settled mainly on the East Coast of the United States. Chinese and Japanese from Asia settled mainly on the West Coast of the United States.

Mexicans came to the southwest, and a large Cuban population has settled in Florida. Puerto Ricans and Haitians can be found in many large East Coast cities. More recently, Vietnamese, Cambodians, and other Asians have settled in many parts of the United States. Each ethnic group has brought its own culture and language to the United States and created its own national **enclaves** in various parts of the country. But each has taken up and improved on the American way of life. Each in its own way has contributed to a distinctly American culture. Many have taken an active part in politics, and the ethnic groups in the

U.S. have found it to their advantage to work with one another.

In Russia, which operated under dictatorship for most of its history, there was little freedom of expression and little interest on the part of the many ethnic groups to work with one another.

Ethnic Russians, those who live mainly in the 6 1/2 million square miles of the Russian republic, made up about 52 percent of the former Soviet Union. They speak the Russian language. The rest of the former Soviet population speaks more than 100 distinct languages and follows numerous faiths, particularly Russian Orthodox. Judaism, Buddhism, and Islam are also widely practiced. The followers of Islam, the Muslims, number more than 45 million in the C.I.S.

Slavs, the Largest Language Group

The Slavs are the largest language group in Eastern Europe. They are divided into three parts: the West Slavs in Poland and Czechoslovakia (now called the Czech and Slovak Federal Republic), the South Slavs in Serbia/Yugoslavia and Bulgaria, and the East Slavs in Russia.

The East Slavs populate the republics of the Ukraine (the people are sometimes called "Little Russians"), Belarus (formerly Byelorussia—the people are sometimes called "White Russians"), and Russia. The East Slavs are the dominant ethnic group in Russia by far, but even among the different Slavic groups there are vast differences in cultural **heritage**.

Troublesome Nationalities

There has always been an underground rumble of trouble among the various republics that made up the former Soviet Union, but tsarist terror and later Communist terror and discipline kept outright fighting to a minimum.

With the collapse of communism, old hatreds have surfaced in many of the republics and sometimes bitter and deadly fighting has broken out between ethnic groups. The Commonwealth of Independent States hopes to play a role in keeping the peace, but in 1992 it was mainly Russian troops, trying to protect ethnic Russians in the various republics, who had intervened in some of the fighting.

The situation was made worse by the presence of large stores of arms left over from the **cold war** and taken over by the newly independent republics.

THE FORMER SOVIET REPUBLICS

Directions:

Number your paper from 1 to 5. Answer the following questions.
1. What is an ethnic group?
2. What is the dominant ethnic group in Russia?
3. Name two differences and two similarities in the ethnic development of the United States and the former Soviet Union.
4. What was the first ethnic group to arrive in America from Europe?
5. Name three ethnic groups who have come to live in the United States.

PART 2:
Russia, the Ukraine, Moldova, and Belarus

Russia, by its size, mineral wealth, and culture history, will always be the leader in any political structure in which it is involved. If democracy and free enterprise succeed in Russia, the other republics will be dragged along because they still depend on the vast resources of Russia.

Russia's "head" borders on the three Baltic republics on the west. Its "heart" is Moscow, its capital, and its "tail" is the port of Vladivostok on the Sea of Japan, about 6,000 miles east of the Baltic republics. Russia, also called "Great Russia," ranges from the crowded cities of Moscow and St. Petersburg to the barren **tundra**, dense forests, and **permafrost** of Siberia.

Russia was the first republic organized after the Bolshevik Revolution of 1917. It was created out of political rather than ethnic considerations, and this division continues to cause trouble. Some distinctly ethnic parts of Russia, particularly the Mongol and Muslim areas, seek independence from Russian authority.

In 1992, Russia had a population of about 150 million. Russia's land area of 6 1/2 million square miles was 76 percent of the land area of the former Soviet Union. Its major ethnic group is Great Russian. Russia produced about 70 percent of the total output of the former Soviet Union. Beneath the frozen wastes of Siberia lie untold amounts of mineral wealth.

Russia was also responsible for more than 70 percent of the agricultural production and had 90 percent of the coal reserves of the former Soviet Union. It had more than that in gold and iron.

Its rail network is a centerpiece for the transportation system in all the former Soviet republics, and despite the breakup of the Soviet Union, Russia continues to provide leadership and strength in many areas.

The Ukraine

The mineral and oil-rich Ukraine is the heartland of ancient Russia and the most densely populated of the former Soviet republics. It had 16 percent of the total population of the former Soviet Union.

The Russian state began in the Ukrainian capital of Kiev, but that city was later destroyed by the Mongol invasion. Although it lost its dominant position to Moscow, Kiev continued to be a mighty political and economic force in the Soviet Union. Now, the two countries—Russia and the Ukraine—must work side by side to make the new democratic system work.

Home of the Cossacks

It was on the Ukrainian **steppes** that millions of colorful Cossack horsemen established their headquarters as an escape from tsarist rule. The Cossacks

Map Study: *This map shows the republics of the former Soviet Union. Which republic is the largest? the second largest? Which republic is south and east of Armenia? Name three republics that border on the Ukraine.*

actually created a government of their own and were a political factor into the twentieth century. Now, with freedom returned to the Ukraine, the Cossacks are once again gathering to make their presence felt.

In World War II, the Ukraine countryside and its people were ravaged during bitter fighting between the German and Soviet armies. The Ukraine became famous for the struggle of its **partisan** armies against the Germans behind German lines.

Breadbasket

The summers are hot and the winters are long and cold, but the soil is **fertile** enough so that the Ukraine earned the name "breadbasket" of the former Soviet Union because of its enormous

This Buryat horseman near Lake Baikal in Siberia is a descendent of Mongolian nomads. Siberia makes up a large part of Great Russia.

Biggest Cities

The largest city in Russia is Moscow. More than eight million people live in the Russian capital, which makes it about the same size as New York City. St. Petersburg (formerly Leningrad) is next with over four million, followed by Kiev, capital of the republic of Ukraine, with over 2.4 million, and Tashkent, capital of the Uzbekistan Republic, with just over two million.

Russia is experiencing a population drain from rural areas to the large cities, where people expect to find more work and goods. The government is trying to provide the rural population with more "social amenities," from televisions to medical care and housing, to encourage people to remain on the farms.

---

production of grain. The fertile black soils (**chernozems**) begin just north of Kiev and continue south almost to the Black Sea. Sugar beets and **livestock** are other important products of this rich republic.

Three great rivers—the Bug, the Dnieper, and the Donets—cross the Ukraine's generally flat **terrain**, providing generous amounts of hydroelectric power to the economy. The basin of the Donets River has large deposits of coal and iron. There are also large deposits of manganese in the Ukraine.

Eighty miles north of Kiev is Chernobyl (cheer NOH bl). Chernobyl was once a city of 12,000 people. On

April 26, 1986, there was an explosion and fire at the nuclear power plant in Chernobyl. It was the world's worst nuclear disaster.

Thirty-one people were killed, and about 135,000 people were evacuated from northern Ukraine and southern Belarus (formerly Byelorussia). Many countries sent medical supplies to the area. Doctors from all over the world who are specialists in treating patients with radiation poisoning have been helping victims of the disaster. Except for security forces and cleanup crews, the city of Chernobyl is empty. Its smoldering reactor is covered by thousands of tons of concrete, but it remains a threat to the surrounding population.

Moldova

To the south of the Ukraine is Moldova (formerly Moldavia). At 13,000 square miles, it was the second smallest of the former Soviet Union republics behind Armenia. Because of its location between Asia and southern Europe and its relatively flat terrain, Moldova for centuries was a pathway for invaders. This has led to a heavy ethnic mix of people.

Moldova is a land of vineyards, orchards, and grain fields sandwiched between Romania on the west and the Ukraine on the east. The republic is primarily a producer of food and consumer goods. It is also a major wine-producing area. It has few natural resources. Its summers are warm and moist; its winters are long, dry, and very cold. January temperatures average well below freezing.

Stalin annexed most of Moldova from Romania after World War II, so more than 60 percent of the Moldovan population is actually ethnic Romanian. Ethnic Russians make up about 13 percent of the population, and these Russians have attempted to create a state separate from Moldova. This led to bloody fighting in 1992.

The Flatlands of Belarus

On the Polish border on the western end of the former Soviet Union is Belarus, the third largest Slavic republic of the former Soviet Union. More than a third of its land is covered by swamps and marsh, especially in the Pripet marshes in the south. The **climate** is cold, with January temperatures averaging below 20 degrees. About 80 percent of the population speaks the White Russian language, a Slavic language closely related to Russian. Belarus was one of the most backward and poverty-stricken areas in Russia before the Bolshevik Revolution in 1917. In the late nineteenth and early twentieth centuries, more than one and a half million people

Commonwealth of Independent States

Republic	Capital	*Area	**Population	Ethnic Groups	Industry, Agriculture
Russia	Moscow	6,590,950	150M	83% Russian	Wood, steel, oil, grain
Belarus	Minsk	80,133	10.1M	Belarus 79%, Russians 12%, Poles 4%	Machinery, tools, textiles, flax, grain
Ukraine	Kiev	233,028	51.4M	Ukrainians 74%, Russians 21%, Jews 1%	Beets, grain, coal, iron, chemicals
Moldova	Kishinev	13,008	4.2M	Moldovans 64%, Ukrainians 14%, Russians 13%	Grain, fruit, wine, textiles
Armenia	Yerevan	11,502	3.5M	Armenians 86%, Azerbaijanis 5%	Copper, zinc, aluminum
Azerbaijan	Baku	33,504	6.8M	Azerbaijanis 78%, Russians 8%	Iron, cobalt, wheat, fruit, oil
Turkmenistan	Ashkhbad	188,406	3.5M	Turkmenians 68%, Russians 13%, Uzbeks 9%	Cotton, corn, carpets, oil, coal, sulfur, salt
Uzbekistan	Tashkent	172,696	19.6M	Uzbeks 68%, Russians 11%, Tatars 4%	Rice, silk, steel, cars, textiles, coal, oil
Tajikistan	Dushanbe	55,236	5M	Tajiks 59%, Uzbeks 23%, Russians 10%	Cotton, grain, rice, fruit, heavy industry, coal
Kyrgyzstan	Frunze	76,621	4.2M	Kyrgyzias 48%, Russians 26%, Uzbeks 12%	Cattle breeding, tobacco, cotton, rice, beets
Kazakhstan	Alma-Ata	1,048,762	16.5M	Kazakhs 36%, Russians 42%, Ukrainians 6%	Coal, oil, iron, tin, copper, zinc
Former Soviet Republics Not Part of C.I.S.					
Estonia	Tallinn	17,408	1.8M	Estonians 65%, Russians 28%	Textiles, shipbuilding, timber, mining, fishing
Latvia	Riga	24,588	2.7M	Latvians 54%, Russians 33%	Timber, peat, electronics
Lithuania	Vilnius	25,167	3.7M	Liths 80%, Russians 9%, Poles 7%	Cattle, hogs, appliances, fishing
Georgia	Tbilisi	26,904	5.3M	Georgians 69%, Armenians 9%, Russians 8%	Timber, coal, textiles, iron, grain, tea, fruit

*Area in square miles   **M = million

Source: Office of the Embassy of Russia

Chart Study: *What is the capital of Belarus? Which republic has an area of 173,200 square miles? Which republic has the smallest population? Is that republic the smallest in terms of land area? Name three republics that became Soviet Socialist Republics in 1922.*

emigrated to other countries, mainly the United States.

It was through Belarus that French armies in the nineteenth century and German armies in the twentieth century moved into the Russian heartland. The region was devastated both times. The fighting and German occupation during World War II (1941-1945) reduced the flat landscape to a virtual desert.

More than three million people were left homeless after the war in that one republic alone.

The republic developed a strong industrial base while part of the Soviet Union. It produced trucks, farm machinery, tools, radios, and motors. Peat is the major mineral resource. It is used as fuel for electric power stations.

Agricultural land is limited, but many marshes have been drained. Belarus is a leading hog-raising area.

R E V I E W

Directions:
Number your paper from 1 to 5. Answer the following questions.
1. What frightening thing occurred at Chernobyl in 1986?
2. What was the first republic to be organized after the Bolshevik Revolution?
3. In what republic do the Cossacks live?
4. Why was Moldova a pathway for invaders?
5. Through what other region did French and German invaders march?

PART 3:
Armenia and Azerbaijan

These are two small republics squeezed between the Caspian Sea on the east and Turkey on the west. Armenia was the smallest of the Soviet republics at 11,500 square miles. The influence of ancestral tribes on Armenian culture is typical of what went on in other Soviet republics. The name of the republic comes from the Armens, a tribe that invaded the area in the seventh century B.C. This tribe imposed its language (somewhat similar to Greek) and its rule on the population.

The long history of the Armenians includes brief periods of independence and many years of domination by various conquerors, primarily the Turks and Russians. Through it all, the Armenians have fiercely preserved their customs, language, and sense of national identity based on their tribal roots. The Armenians gained world-wide attention during and shortly after World War I because of brutal **massacres** of its population by the Turks. Millions of dollars were raised in the United States and elsewhere to help the "starving Armenians."

Armenia is mountainous and **prone**

to damaging and deadly earthquakes. It is cold in winter and hot and dry during its brief summers. Cotton, tobacco, and fruit are the main agricultural products. Armenian wine is known throughout Europe.

Armenia's many industries include electronics, machinery, machine tools, textiles, and canning. It is a major producer of copper. It also mines zinc, iron, gold, and silver.

Azerbaijan, Major Oil Producer

Armenia's neighbor to the east is Azerbaijan (as uhr BY jahn). This independent republic features the high mountains of the Caucasus range, broad plains, and semideserts. It has a cold climate except for the area that borders on the Caspian Sea, where it is usually mild and **humid**.

Azerbaijan is an important producer of oil. It was a target of Hitler's armies

Oil from Azerbaijan is often shipped out of Georgia's port of Batumi on the Black Sea.

in World War II when the Germans launched a major drive through the Caucasus Mountains to capture the oil fields. They did capture parts of the fields, but the Russians did such a thorough job of destroying the oil-drilling equipment that the Germans were unable to obtain much oil from the fields.

Much of Azerbaijan's industry is based on agricultural products, such as cotton and silk milling, canning, and meat processing. The republic was the second leading cotton grower in the former Soviet Union, next to Uzbekistan. It also produces citrus fruits, wheat, and vegetables. Azerbaijan also contains many minerals.

Christianity came to Azerbaijan in the second century. The republic is said to be the site of the legendary Garden of Eden. Azerbaijan has been fought over for centuries and was conquered by the Persians (Iranians), Turks, and Russians. Today, more than half the population is made up of Azerbaijan Turks. The republic has a large Muslim population, and this has been the root of a simmering war between Christian Armenia and mostly Muslim Azerbaijan.

Even before the breakup of the Soviet Union, the two republics were fighting for control of Nagorno-Karabakh, a Christian Armenian area entirely inside Muslim Azerbaijan. The fighting grew worse in 1992, with several thousand people dying in bitter combat. The situation was made worse by the large numbers of tanks, warplanes, guns, and ammunition left under the republics' control after the breakup of the Soviet Union.

R E V I E W

Directions:
Number your paper from 1 to 5. Answer the following questions.
1. Which republic was the smallest of the former Soviet republics?
2. Why was Azerbaijan a major target of Hitler's armies in World War II?
3. What drew international attention to Armenia during and shortly after World War I?
4. What natural disaster sometimes strikes Armenia?
5. Azerbaijanis are mostly of what religion?

PART 4:
The Republics of Central Asia

The five republics in Central Asia include Kazakhstan (kuh zak STAN), land of the Russian steppes (generally flat and grassy), and the remote and mountainous Kyrgyzstan (cur giz STAN) on the Chinese border. The other Central Asian republics are Tajikistan (tah jeek i STAN), Turkmenistan (tuhrk muhn i STAN), and Uzbekistan (uhz behk i STAN). They all have similar ethnic backgrounds.

Much of the population of these five republics is descended from Turkic-Mongol ancestors, traditionally nomadic herdsmen who drove their cattle from place to place in search of food and water. Their religion and culture is Muslim. Shepherds still tend their flocks and a few **nomads** continue to roam this land of small villages and large farms. They live a life remote in every way from the bustling cities of western Russia.

With the exception of Kazakhstan, these republics have been the most resistant to change since the breakup of the Soviet Union in December 1991. Former Communists still hold power in their governments, and democracy and free enterprise have been slow to take hold.

THE FORMER SOVIET REPUBLICS

The Second Largest Republic

Of the former Soviet republics, Kazakhstan is second in land area only to Russia. It extends from the Caspian Sea on the southwest to the Chinese border on the east. Below zero temperatures are common in winter, and it is windy in any season, especially on the flat steppe land.

It was in Kazakhstan that the Mongols made their headquarters during their **domination** of Russia in the thirteenth and fourteenth centuries. Centuries later, Kazakhs (the people of Kazakhstan) regularly rebelled against their tsarist masters, and it took the Communists more than seven years to establish control in the region after the 1917 Bolshevik Revolution.

Kazakhstan's industry and **agriculture** were greatly developed by the Soviet government. Since World War II, the republic has been transformed from a backward, livestock-raising region into a modern agricultural and industrial state. Of particular importance is the use of crop irrigation in the rich but moisture-poor land.

Kazakhstan is rich in minerals, producing large amounts of copper, lead, iron, and zinc. Among its more than 25,000 industrial enterprises are many chemical producers. Kazakhstan has been particularly hard-hit by the breakup of the Soviet Union and the move to free

Kyrgyzia nomads rest near Bukhara in Uzbekistan.

enterprise. Many of its industries operated at a loss and were supported by the Soviet government to keep them going. Under the free enterprise system, the industries have to make it by doing a better job than their competitors, not with government money.

Turkmenistan and the Vast Kara Kum

To the southwest of Kazakhstan is the republic of Turkmenistan. At its western end, Turkmenistan borders on the Caspian Sea. About 85 percent of the country is made up of the **Kara Kum**, a vast and forbidding desert region and the driest area in the C.I.S. Most of the population lives in river valleys and **oases**. Cotton is the leading crop. An attempt has been made to improve the crop-growing ability of the region with extensive **irrigation**.

The republic has great deposits of salt, and also produces gypsum, oil, phosphate, and limestone.

Kyrgyzstan and Tajikistan

The earthquake-prone republics of Kyrgyzstan and Tajikistan huddle next to each other on the southern border of the former Soviet Union. Both have winters that are bitterly cold.

Kyrgyzstan is a country of high mountains and deep gorges. Its **terrain** is dominated by the Tien Shan Mountains, which range up to 24,000-plus feet. (The Pamir Mountains in eastern Tajikistan also tower above 24,000 feet). The Kyrgyzias, an ancient Turkic-Mongol race, have been a nomadic people for centuries, with a strong tribal background that continues to this day. Much of the cropland is now irrigated, and grains and cotton are the main crops. The republic is also a leading producer of mercury.

Tajikistan, noted for the permanent **glaciers** that adorn parts of its Pamir Mountain range, has a mainly agricultural economy. Its principal crop is cotton, grown by irrigation. The republic's industries include mining and food processing. Rapid run-off from melting snow on the mountain peaks helps the republic to be a major producer of cheap hydroelectric power.

Uzbekistan

Uzbekistan to the west is a major Muslim republic. Much of its population descends from the Turkic and Arab nomads who once roamed the country. Tamarlane, the Mongol conqueror who once ruled major regions of Asia, made Samarkand, in what is now Uzbekistan, his capital.

The southeastern half of the republic is **fertile** and heavily populated. The northwestern part is mostly desert. Uzbekistan has brief, cold winters and long, dry summers. It is a large grower of rice and cotton. It also has many orchards.

Industry grew rapidly during World War II as the Soviet government moved factories and workers beyond the reach of German armies. Much of its industry produces fertilizer and farm equipment. Uzbekistan also has abundant mineral reserves, including copper, petroleum, tungsten, and lead.

THE FORMER SOVIET REPUBLICS

R
E
V
I
E
W

Directions:
Number your paper from 1 to 5. Answer the following questions.
1. What are the five republics that are grouped as Central Asian republics?
2. Of what religion are most of the people in the five republics?
3. What is the name of the huge desert in Turkmenistan?
4. How has melting snow helped the economy of Tajikistan?
5. Why did the Soviet government move many factories to Uzbekistan during World War II?

PART 5:
The Baltic States and Georgia

The Baltic states of Lithuania, Latvia, and Estonia began to agitate for independence at the first signs of Soviet decline. Lithuania was the leader of this movement, and on March 11, 1990, declared its independence from the Soviet Union. What followed was nearly two years of argument and bloodshed before the three republics finally were free.

The Baltic states, in the area between the East Slavs of Russia and the Western countries, have a long history of independence. The Lithuanians especially were a powerful force in the fourteenth and fifteenth centuries. In 1940, Soviet armies marched into the states and declared them Soviet Socialist Republics.

They were occupied by Germany for part of World War II, but were reclaimed by the Soviet Union in 1944. All of the political opponents of communism were imprisoned or killed, and many thousands died. The Soviets imposed their language and government on the Baltic states as part of an intense **Russification** program. However, these states continued to have a basically Western culture.

Agricultural products, machinery, and other industrial goods from the Baltic states were important to the Soviet economy. In return, the Soviets supplied the states with oil and coal at low prices.

A Major Test

Lithuania was a major test for Soviet President Mikhail Gorbachev and his attempts to keep the Soviet Union together. He tried to make an example of

SPOTLIGHT
S T O R Y

Down on the Farm

What do you think is the largest area of cooperation between the United States and Russia?

The first thing that might come to mind is space, where U.S. and Russian astronauts have conducted joint experiments. But the largest area of cooperation is actually down on the farm, where U.S. experts are helping Russia and other republics of the Commonwealth of Independent States to grow more food. Much of the help is in the form of training programs and advice for Russian farmers.

The republics of the C.I.S. are the largest growers of wheat in the world, yet they are also the leading buyers of grain, corn, and soybeans from the United States. And their people still have to stand in long lines for bread.

It might be in the best financial interests of American farmers for Russia to continue buying large amounts of agricultural products from them. However, government officials and private companies in the United States continue to help the Russians in farming, livestock-raising, and food processing. They do this for political as well as humanitarian reasons. Many feel that helping Russia in this way will help save democracy there and eventually provide even larger markets for American goods.

The Russians love the land. Farmers working in their fields is a sight as old and traditional as the country itself. Many teachers, workers, and students will leave the city during harvest time to help farmers bring in the crops. Even scientists, physicists, and engineers, all near the top of Russian society, may work for several days each year in the fields. Some do it for extra money and food, some volunteer because they like it, and others, like the military, have been ordered into the fields. This practice is so widespread and necessary that it has become part of the Russian culture.

Stop and Review

Write the answers to these questions on your paper.

1. What is the largest area of cooperation between the United States and Russia?
2. Why does the U.S. help Russian farmers?
3. In what two areas does the U.S. help Russian farmers?
4. What three products does Russia buy from the United States?
5. For what reasons does the average Russian citizen work in the fields?

Windmills, like these just outside of Kiev, are still important to farmers.

These Ukrainian farm workers are visiting the city of Lvov in the Ukraine to do some shopping.

get. It was a turning point not only in the affairs of the Baltic states, but in the fate of the Soviet Union as well.

Later in the year, seven Lithuanian border guards were murdered by Russian "black beret" riot troops in an attempt to provoke Lithuanian resistance, and thus give the Russians an excuse to send in more troops. Again, world leaders denounced Soviet actions, and Gorbachev could see that it was all over.

that country by sending in troops to threaten the Lithuanian leadership. That leadership stood fast and non-violently against the Soviets while Gorbachev tried to work out a compromise. Lithuania wanted no compromise—it wanted its freedom. Meanwhile, Gorbachev was caught between the hard-line Communists who wanted things to remain as they were, and the **radicals**, led by Boris Yeltsin, who believed that each nationality should determine its own future.

Gorbachev responded to the hardliners, and on January 13, 1991, Russian troops attacked Lithuanian citizens defending a television station in the capital of Vilnius. Fourteen citizens were killed and 163 injured. The world was horrified at a time when Gorbachev needed all the foreign support he could

New Names

The revulsion against the old days of Communist leadership have resulted in a number of name changes of some cities and republics.

The name changes of some of the republics reflect a return to ethnic beginnings. For instance, Moldavia was changed to Moldova. Moldavia was the Russian spelling of the country. Moldova is the Romanian spelling and reflects the fact that a majority of Moldovans are ethnic Romanians.

Other changes in the names of the republics: Byelorussia became Belarus; Kirghizia is now Kyrgyzstan; Tadzhikistan is Tajikistan, and Turkmenia is Turkmenistan.

Two major cities underwent name changes along with many smaller cities. Leningrad, named after the leader of the 1917 Bolshevik Revolution, resumed its former name of St. Petersburg. Sverdlovsk, home of Russian President Boris Yeltsin, became Yekaterinburg.

The courage of the Baltic states had won, and in the latter part of 1991, Gorbachev granted them full independence. A few months later, the Soviet Union fell to pieces, and Gorbachev was out of power.

Climate, Agriculture, and Industry

The climate of the Baltic states is cold in the winter and warm and wet during the brief summers. Estonia's climate is moderated somewhat by its location on the Gulf of Finland. Agriculture and cattle-raising are an important part of the economy of the Baltic states. Estonia is a land of forest, meadows, swamps, and **moors**. It also has a thriving fishing industry.

Latvia, on the Baltic Sea, has many lakes, small streams, **peat bogs**, and rich oil shale deposits. Its population is almost two-thirds Lettish, a nationality group. The Letts, with the Lithuanians, form a linguistic group known as the Baltic Group. In other words, the Liths and Latvians more or less speak the same language.

The Estonian language is from an entirely different language group called Finno-Ugric, which is similar to the language spoken by natives of the country of Finland. (Finland is to the north of Estonia). Estonia and Latvia are mostly Protestant. Lithuania is more than 75 percent Roman Catholic.

The Baltic states became much more industrialized under Soviet rule. Latvia, like Lithuania, has a large machine-building industry. The Latvians produce electrical equipment and farm machinery among other industrial products. Estonia's major industries are food processing (especially fish) and the processing of oil shale.

Georgia

To see a truly multi-cultural state, you should go to Georgia in the southwestern part of the former Soviet Union. There, you would meet its colorful, fun-loving citizens, who are known to excel in fighting, hunting, and athletics.

The Georgians are descendants of an ancient and civilized culture that extends back to at least 3000 B.C. Many Georgians are dark-haired and bushy-browed. Some have large noses, of which they are proud. By the nature of their outgoing personalties and physical characteristics, they usually stand out in any crowd.

Georgia is the birthplace of many leading writers and intellectuals. Natives of Georgia include the late Soviet dictator, Joseph Stalin, and Laurentia Beria. Beria was chief of the secret police under Stalin. He was executed during a power struggle following the death of Stalin in 1953.

Georgians take a keen interest in the

arts and sciences. The republic is sprinkled with lively theater and dance groups, including the State Folk Dance Company. This group has made several world tours. Georgia also has an important film industry, as well as outstanding opera and ballet companies in all its major cities. The state library system extends to some of the smallest villages. An important milestone in Georgian cultural life was the founding in 1941 of the Academy of Sciences of Georgia. This academy groups together more than 50 scientific and research institutes.

Georgia is a land of great **contrast**. It ranges from the snow-capped Caucasus mountain range in the north to the subtropical region along the Black Sea, where palm trees grow in abundance. Its Black Sea resorts are a favorite vacation spot for foreigners as well as Russians.

Although there has been much industrial growth since World War II, Georgia's economy is still basically agricultural. Georgia has rich crop and grazing lands, extensive tea plantations, vineyards, and citrus orchards. Some enterprising Georgian businessmen have been known to pack their suitcases with tomatoes, fruit, and strawberries and fly into big cities where shoppers will pay high prices for fresh produce.

Georgia has great mineral wealth, particularly coal and manganese. Its industry produces steel, fertilizers, trucks and other industrial products.

From 1922 to 1936, Georgia, along with Armenia and Azerbaijan, formed the Transcaucasian Republic. When this republic was dissolved, the three became separate republics in the Soviet Union.

Trouble Within

Georgia has always been independence-minded, and in April of 1991, voters in the republic went to the polls and voted overwhelmingly for independence. This was not accepted by the Soviet leadership, which pleaded with the Georgian leaders to wait and join a new union that Gorbachev was trying to form. The Georgians weren't interested. When the Soviet Union fell apart in December 1991, the Georgians refused—along with the Baltic states—to become a part of the Commonwealth of Independent States.

Independence was not kind to Georgia through most of 1992. Its first elected president was a scoundrel who wanted to set up a dictatorship. He was driven from office and holed up in the western mountains of Georgia to continue his warfare against Georgian leaders.

Then, early in 1992, fighting broke out in a region called South Ossetia, which wanted to secede from Georgia.

Troops were sent to stop the secession. Several people were killed and the fighting continued.

In August 1992, the region of Abkhasia declared its independence from Georgia, which sent thousands of troops to restore order. Before the breakup of the Soviet Union, Abkhasia was an autonomous republic in the west of Georgia. Now it wanted to form its own country and its parliament declared the country's independence.

R E V I E W

Directions:
Number your paper from 1 to 5. Answer the following questions.
1. What are the names of the three Baltic states? Describe how they became part of the Soviet Union.
2. What are some of the ethnic differences between the Baltic states?
3. Of what religion are most of the people of Lithuania?
4. What remains the basis of Georgia's economy?
5. What troubles has Georgia had since it gained independence?

THE FORMER SOVIET REPUBLICS

MAP SKILLS

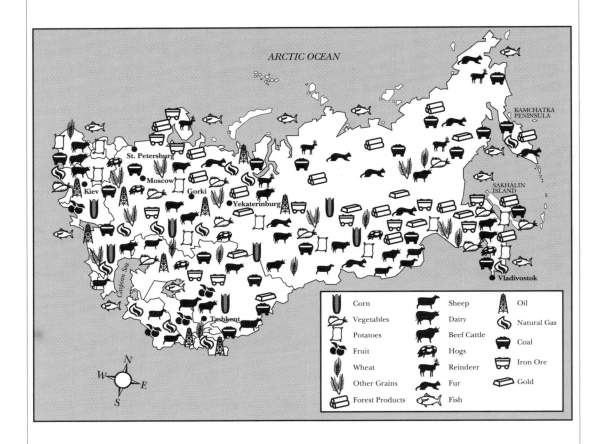

PRODUCT MAP OF THE FORMER SOVIET UNION

Directions:

Number your paper from 1 to 8. Use the map on this page to help you answer the following questions.

1. What symbol does this map use for dairy products?
2. Name two crops grown near the Caspian Sea.
3. Name two kinds of livestock that are raised just north of Kiev.
4. Are there more reindeer in the northern or southern parts of Russia?
5. Name two kinds of natural resources near Vladivostok.
6. Name three products that can be found on the Kamchatka Peninsula.
7. Would you be more likely to find hog farms near Tashkent or St. Petersburg?
8. What kind of mining takes place near St. Petersburg?

CHAPTER 3 REVIEW

Summary of the Former Soviet Republics

The former Soviet Union is now 15 separate and independent countries. Eleven of the former Soviet republics joined in a loose union called the Commonwealth of Independent States. More than 100 distinct languages are spoken in these former Soviet republics. Many religious faiths are followed.

The largest of the former Soviet republics is Russia, also called Great Russia. It had more than half the population and about three-quarters of the land area of the old Soviet Union. It produced more than 70 percent of the agricultural and industrial output. All types of climate are represented in the former republics of the Soviet Union.

Many of the republics are rich in mineral wealth. The Baltic states of Lithuania, Latvia, and Estonia and the republic of Georgia chose not to join the Commonwealth of Independent States. Georgia has had many problems since it became independent. Some parts of it are trying to secede from Georgia, and there has been much fighting.

Critical Thinking Skills

Directions: Give some serious thought to the questions below. Be sure to answer in complete sentences.

1. Consider your own ethnic background. What is it? How many people of other ethnic backgrounds do you know?
2. What are some special cultural things that you practice or have learned from your parents that are related to your ethnic background?
3. Which former Soviet republic would you like to live in if you had your choice? Why?
4. What are some problems that can occur in a country with many different languages?

For Discussion

Directions: Discuss these questions with your class. Appoint one class member to write on the board the ideas you discover.

1. If you could visit the republics of the former Soviet Union, which one would you most like to visit? Why?
2. Discuss some of the ways you think climate has affected the citizens of Russia and the other republics.
3. Why did the nationality problem cause so much trouble in the Soviet Union?

Write It!

Directions: You work for a travel agency. Write an ad for one of the republics that you think would lead Americans to visit there.

For You to Do

Directions: You are a farmer in the republic of the Ukraine, a rich farming area. You want to grow crops in addition to wheat and sugar beets, which are favored by Ukrainian farmers but provide a lot of competition to your own crop. The growing season in the Ukraine is about 150 days, and the average temperature during this time ranges from 58 degrees to about 69 degrees Fahrenheit. Annual rainfall averages 26 inches. Go to the library and find out what crops might do well under these conditions. Based on your findings, what crops would you grow other than wheat and sugar beets?

THE ARTS AND SCIENCES

- There are more than 900 museums in the Commonwealth of Independent States.
- The former Soviet Union launched the world's first Earth satellite in 1957.
- Russia has the world's highest ratio of doctors to population.
- The former Soviet Union launched the first unmanned spacecraft to land on Venus.

PART 1:
Music and Literature

Can you imagine great Russian music being featured by symphony orchestras at Fourth of July celebrations in the United States?

That is exactly what happens every year at concerts all over America. The powerful *1812 Overture* written in 1881 was a tribute to Russia's great victory over Napoleon. The overture is often played to the thunder of fireworks to help celebrate our own independence.

The Great Composers

Other music by Pyotr Ilich Tchaikovsky (Chi KOV sky) (1840-1893) is considered among the greatest compositions in the world. His great **ballets** are *Swan Lake, The Nutcracker* and *Sleeping Beauty. The Nutcracker* is about Christmas toys that come alive at night. It is still loved by audiences everywhere, especially during the Christmas season. Even after 100 years, Tchaikovsky's bal-

Violinist Vladimir Spivakov directs the "Virtuosos of Moscow." Classical music is quite popular in the C.I.S.

lets, symphonies, and **operas** remain overwhelming favorites of music lovers in America. He is just one example of the great Russian composers, writers, and artists who have lived since the eighteenth century.

The works of many other Russian composers are still popular today. Sergey Prokofiev (pruh KOF yuhf) (1891-1953) is famous for his *Peter and the Wolf.* Sergey Rachmaninoff (rach man i NOFF) (1873-1943) was a renowned composer, pianist, and conductor whose work reflected the melancholy and gloom of Russian life under the **tsars**. The music of Aram Khachaturian (kahch uh TUHR ee uhn) (1903-1978) illustrates the fire and vitality of Russian life.

Dmitry Shostakovich (shahs tuh KOH vich) (1906-1975) has a special place in Russian hearts. This brooding composer was sharply criticized by Communist authorities who called his music "trash" because it didn't follow the **party line** closely enough for them.

There is little that is light-hearted in Russian art, music, and literature. The emotions are deeply felt and reflect the love and concern that its people have for their country.

The Great Writers

Russian literature, like its music, reflects the same deep understanding of the country and its troubles. The works of its great poets and writers are still read today.

Alexsandr Pushkin (1799-1837) is remembered for his poem *Eugene Onegrin* and his historical drama *Boris Godonov.*

Fyodor Dostoyevski (1821-1881), a **liberal** thinker who was exiled to Siberia in the 1840s, focused on the darkest themes in human nature. His classic *Crime and Punishment* is about a man who murders a woman for her money. It includes the innermost thoughts of the unfortunate criminal who was caught after committing the crime.

Dostoyevski also wrote *Memoirs from the House of the Dead,* which was about his experiences while in **exile** in Siberia; *The Brothers Karamazov,* about a father who is murdered by his sons; and *The Idiot,* about the place of a righteous and honest man in the world.

Nikolay Gogol (1809-1852) wrote about the deadly system of serfdom under the **tsars** in the novel *Dead Souls*. In his comedy *The Inspector General*, Gogol made fun of clumsy Russian officials.

Count Leo Tolstoy (1828-1910) came from a wealthy family but attacked the government's treatment of the lower classes in much of his writing. His epic novel *War and Peace* is about the lives of the Russian upper classes during the invasion of Russia by Napoleon in 1812. The Russian public still treasures this account of old Russia and many Russians can recite long passages from its pages. Tolstoy also wrote *Anna Karenina*, a gripping novel of love, humiliation, and death. These themes are typical of Russian literature.

Anton Chekhov (1860-1904) is the best-known of the Russian playwrights. Many of his plays, including *Uncle Vanya*, *The Three Sisters*, and *The Cherry Orchard*, are still performed all over the world.

The Value of the Theater

The theater was permitted some freedom under the tsars to produce plays with liberal trends, but this ended when the Bolsheviks took over the country in 1917. The Bolsheviks recognized the

The Moscow Academic Vladimir Mayakovsky Theatre performs a scene from the play **The Sunset***.*

value of the theater as a major **propaganda** tool. (This was before radio and television; movies were just getting started). Plays were produced only to further the interests of the Communist party. All theaters were placed under government control and remained there until the Communist party was driven from power.

Control over subject matter in the plays that could be shown was gradually relaxed under Soviet leader Mikhail Gorbachev from 1985 to the end of 1991. With the breakup of the Soviet Union in 1991 and the creation of the Commonwealth of Independent States, all these matters are under the control of the individual republics. Control now ranges from none to some, depending on the republic.

The Russians have made great contributions to the dramatic arts.

THE ARTS AND SCIENCES

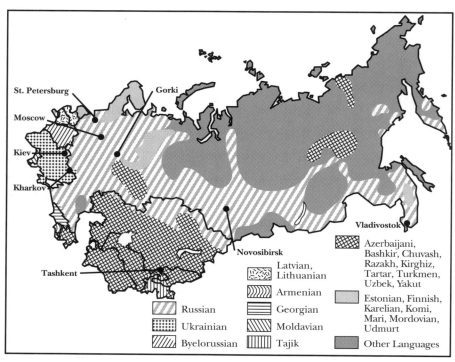

Map Study: *This map shows where different languages are spoken. Name five languages that are spoken in Tashkent. Name two cities where Ukrainian is spoken. Name five cities where Russian is the main language.*

Konstantin Stanislavsky (1863-1938) created a form of acting known as **method acting**. It has been widely taught in the United States. Actor Marlon Brando uses method acting.

Modern Russian Writers

Among the modern writers are Maxim Gorky (1868-1936), Boris Pasternak (1890-1960), and Aleksandr Solzhenitsyn (1918-).

Gorky's most famous play, *The Lower Depths,* is about the victims of an unjust (in this case tsarist) society. Gorky favored the Bolshevik revolution at first because he was bitterly opposed to the cruelties of tsarist rule. However, he later distanced himself from the Communists when the party's own murderous traits became apparent.

Among the most beloved of all Russian writers is Boris Pasternak, who wrote *Dr. Zhivago,* a story of two lovers caught up in the Russian civil war and eventually crushed by it. Pasternak won the **Nobel Prize** for literature in 1958 for

Dr. Zhivago. However, he was not popular with Communist authorities and was not allowed out of the country to accept the prize.

Aleksandr Solzhenitsyn exposed the terror of Stalin's labor camps with the novel *One Day in the Life of Ivan Denisovich* and his three-volume work *The Gulag Archipelago.* Solzhenitsyn was a captain in the army and was imprisoned in a labor camp for eight years after writing a letter to a friend. In the letter he made a joking reference to Stalin's famous mustache and was imprisoned.

After his release from the labor camp he courageously continued to criticize the Communists in his writings. He was ordered to leave Russia by the Communist party and now lives in the United States. He was later invited back to Russia to live but declined.

Many of the themes in Russian literature are **universal**. Russian literature

This eternal flame in Kiev is dedicated to the victims of Nazi Germany, including the more than 34,000 Jews who were massacred by the Nazis at Babi Yar. Poet Yevgeny Yevtushenko brought Babi Yar to the attention of the world in 1961 when he wrote a poem of the same name mourning the victims and attacking Soviet anti-Semitism. (The government had announced plans to build a sports stadium on the site of Babi Yar.)

has been enjoyed and appreciated by people from many different cultures. Several books including *The Inspector General, Anna Karenina, Crime and Punishment,* and *War and Peace* have been made into movies and are available on video tape.

REVIEW

Directions:
Number your paper from 1 to 5. Answer the following questions.
1. What was the theme of Boris Pasternak's award-winning work?
2. Whose work was called "trash" by the Communists?
3. How did the Bolsheviks use the theater to help their cause?
4. In what ways do you think Russian literature showed resistance to tsarist and Communist governments?
5. How has Russian theater and literature changed under the new governments?

SPOTLIGHT
S T O R Y

The Moscow Circus

The Moscow Circus was a colorful example of the cultural exchanges between the United States and the former Soviet Union. Even in the 1960s, when the two countries were engaged in the **cold war**, the Moscow Circus came regularly to the United States to thrill and perform for millions of Americans. In 1989, the Moscow Circus toured 16 U.S. cities and put on more than 200 shows.

In the Russia of today, the circus is considered an art form on the level of the ballet, opera, and theater. Lenin himself considered the circus so important that in 1919 he directed that the Moscow Circus become part of the government. Until recently, its 6,000 performers were paid by the state. In addition to salaries, the performers received special privileges like roomy apartments, cars, and access to the best food and clothing.

It is uncertain how the Circus will fare under the **market economy** now being developed in Russia, but it is too popular to be done away with. Russians have a special love for the circus. There are more than 150 circus companies in Russia.

The Moscow Circus is like other circuses the world over, with high-wire and trapeze acts, animal acts, clowns, and comedy. But the performers practice long hours and are perfect at what they do. Second-rate performers are not tolerated.

Russians love bears, and Moscow Circus trainers are especially good with them. Years ago, there were acts on big city street corners with bears doing their tricks. And, of course, there are the lions and tigers. Russians are among the best in the world at training these beasts and putting them through intricate performances.

Stop and review

Write the answers to these questions on your paper.

1. The Moscow Circus is an example of what relationship between the United States and the former Soviet Union (now the Commonwealth of Independent States)?
2. How do the Russian people feel about the circus?
3. How were the Moscow Circus performers treated under the government of the Soviet Union?
4. What are some similarities between the Moscow Circus and other circuses around the world?
5. What one animal would you be most likely to see in the Moscow Circus?

Vacheslav Zolkin (center) and his friend, Knopa the bear, delight audiences at the Moscow Circus. Among other things, Knopa knows how to juggle with his feet.

PART 2:
Art, Film, and Ballet

Marc Chagall (shuh GAHL) (1887-1985) is considered by many art experts as the greatest modern Russian artist. He was born in the small Russian-Jewish village of Vitebsk in 1887. At the age of 23, he went to Paris to work and study art, and developed a dream-like painting style that brought him to the top rank of twentieth century artists.

His paintings feature things like large bunches of bright-colored flowers, down-in-the-mouth clowns, and fantastic animals. Images from his childhood, such as fiddlers on roofs and village life, are often reflected in his work. During World War II he and his family fled to the United States from France to escape the Nazis.

Much Russian art tends toward historic and heroic themes on a grand scale. Some of its artists, like Chagall and Vasili Kandinsky, were leaders in the world of modern art during the 1920s and 1930s. Vera Mukhina specialized in monuments and sculptures. Nikolay Roerich painted exotic landscapes and designed monumental historical sets for the stage.

Nationalities and Folk Art

The diverse nationalities and **cultures** of the Russian people produce a vast array of folk and decorative art. Carpets woven in Turkmenistan and other Central Asian republics are valued all over the world. The Lapps of Lapland in the northwestern part of Russia are skilled craftsmen with bone and leather. The Tatars, a race of Mongolian descent who inhabit much of the southern part of Russia, are known for their unusual **architecture**.

Films are Popular

Films are the most popular art form in the Commonwealth of Independent States. There are more than 60,000

Russian craftsmen have a tradition of selling their works at fairs in nearby villages and towns.

movie houses in the Commonwealth. An average film is said to reach more than 15 million viewers at prices much lower than are charged in other countries.

Movies were mainly a **propaganda** tool for the Communist party until the death of Stalin in 1953, when controls were gradually relaxed. Their major emphasis was on the heroic struggles of the working man. The Russian film industry has also produced long, monumental works with historical themes, like *War and Peace* and *The Battleship Potemkin*, a true story in which sailors revolted against tsarist rule.

Government control over the movies gradually declined in the 1980s and disappeared altogether with the collapse of communism and the creation of the Commonwealth of Independent States. There are still those who would return control of all forms of public communication to the government, but the day has passed when this could happen.

Movie themes now focus on family life, problems of living in Russia, crime, and the boredom of life in a country that is still trying to find the right path.

An Elegant Way of Dancing

The ballet is not native to Russia, but it was the Russians who developed it to a degree that made the world aware of its beauty. Ballet, which dates to sixteenth

A World of Romance

Russians are sentimental and emotional when it comes to the arts. They love the sad compositions of Tchaikovsky and his fairy-tale ballets like *Swan Lake* and *The Sleeping Beauty*, because these works take them out of the real world and into the world of romance.

The greater the glories of the lost age of royalty and the tsars and the greater the sweet sadness of music, the better the Russians like it.

century Italy, is a highly **complex**, refined, and **elegant** way of dancing that requires great control and physical strength. The dancing is accompanied by music, colorful costumes, and bright scenery.

Anna Pavlova (1881-1931) and Vaslav Nijinsky (1890-1950) were the two Russian dancers who truly brought ballet to the world. Ballet in the West was enriched by the emigration of Russian dancers such as Rudolph Nureyev (1938-1993) and Mikhail Baryshnikov. Today, Russian dancers continue the **tradition** that makes Russian ballet the best in the world.

There are more than 30 major ballet companies in Russia and the other republics of the C.I.S. The best-known are the Bolshoi Opera and Ballet (bolshoi means "big" in English) on

Sverdlov Square in Moscow and the Kirov Ballet in St. Petersburg. These companies and the Moiseyev Folk Dancers have toured the United States for many years and played to sold-out auditoriums.

The Bolshoi is famous all over the world for **elaborate** productions of the classics and children's ballets. The company's **heritage** goes back to the 1770s, the time of American independence. Like other professional groups, performers for many of the leading dance and theater companies were paid by the Soviet government. They also received special privileges. This is all changing under the new forms of government emerging in the former Soviet Union. The professional groups and the performers will now have to earn their way under a market economy. Their livelihood will depend strictly on the number of paying customers they can attract to their shows.

R E V I E W

Directions:
Number your paper from 1 to 5. Answer the following questions.
1. What themes are important in Russian art?
2. How did the Communists in the former Soviet Union use the movies?
3. What themes do movies in Russia now emphasize?
4. Describe Marc Chagall's style of painting.
5. How do you think the death of Stalin affected the arts?

PART 3:
Russia as a Giant Museum

Russians love the old ways. This love is reflected in the large number of fine **museums** in the country. Many, like the Hermitage in St. Petersburg, are treasure houses of European and Asian art.

Historic St. Petersburg

St. Petersburg was the center of Russian culture in the 200 years before the Bolshevik Revolution. Its large number of museums, monuments, churches, and cathedrals reflect this. Writers like

THE ARTS AND SCIENCES

A piece of rock crystal presented to Tsar Alexander I by the Japanese emperor is one of many items on display in St. Petersburg's Mining Museum.

Pushkin, Gogol, and Dostoyevski lived there, as well as the composers Tchaikovsky, Rimsky-Korsakov, and Shostakovich among others.

Many are buried in the graveyard of the Alexander Nevsky Lavra, one of four monasteries in St. Petersburg. The monastery itself is one of the major sights in St. Petersburg. It has 12 churches and several chapels, all surrounded by walls and **moats**.

Also in St. Petersburg is the world-famous Hermitage. It is connected to the enormous 700-room Winter Palace on the banks of the Neva River. Catherine the Great built the Hermitage as a court museum in 1764. She used it as a private gallery for the art treasures she collected. In the mid-nineteenth century, Tsar Nicholas I had the Hermitage reconstructed and opened to the public. Today, masterpieces of European painting, Russian and Oriental art, ancient Greek and Roman sculpture, as well as many other items, are on display.

Throughout St. Petersburg, there are numerous memorials to that city's struggle against the German armies in World War II. St. Petersburg—then called Leningrad—was virtually surrounded by the Nazis for 900 days. It is estimated that more than a million citizens of the city died of starvation, cold, and disease. The bodies of many of these victims are buried in a mass grave in St. Petersburg. The graveyard has become a national shrine.

The Kremlin

When people think of Russia, they think of the Kremlin and Red Square. Moscow is the center of Russian government. The Kremlin—which means "fortress"—is the centerpiece of Russia. It sits on a small hill overlooking the Moscow River. Nineteen wall towers, once used in the defense of the Kremlin, ring the huge walls. These walls are more than a mile and a quarter in **circumference**. Inside the Kremlin's thick, high walls are masterpieces of ancient cathedrals and churches converted to museums by the Communists after the Bolshevik Revolution. What fate awaits them now that the Communist state has ended no one knows as yet.

Also within the walls of the Kremlin is the Grand Kremlin Palace, built in the middle of the nineteenth century. This mostly houses government offices and reception rooms. Sessions of the **Supreme Soviet**, a legislative body, are also held in the Grand Kremlin Palace. Of special interest inside the Kremlin is the Bell Tower of Ivan the Great, built in the fifteenth century. The Tsar's Bell, also known as the King of Bells, is in front of the tower. At 200 tons, it is the largest bell in the world. It was cast in the seventeenth century.

Also inside the walls of the Kremlin is the Uspensky Sobor, or Assumption Cathedral, traditional site of the **coronation** of tsars. Every tsar from the fifteenth century on was crowned there. This cathedral, with its five golden domes, was built in the fifteenth century.

A view of Red Square: Lenin's tomb is the low building to the left. The State Historical Museum is in the background to the right.

The fantastic Cathedral of St. Basil, built by Ivan the Terrible in the mid-sixteenth century, is just outside the walls of the Kremlin and dominates the landscape. It is now a museum. The rounded domes of St. Basil and of other cathedrals and churches reflect the Mongol-Oriental architectural **heritage** of Russia.

Red Square

On the east side of the Kremlin is Red Square. It is nine football fields long and almost as wide as two football fields. Red Square was site of many historic episodes and the scene of bloody battles during the Bolshevik Revolution.

When the Communists were in power, great military and sports parades were held there to show off Soviet might. Red Square is also the home of the State Historical Museum, formerly an Orthodox church, and the famous

GUM department store, built in the late nineteenth century.

The best-known attraction on Red Square is Lenin's tomb. Millions of Russians and thousands of tourists would stand in long lines each year to view the body of the man who led the Bolshevik Revolution. Now that the Communist state has ended and statues of Lenin have come down throughout much of the country, there is talk of moving Lenin's tomb to a lesser place of honor.

All of this only begins to touch the cultural and scientific importance of Moscow. The city has nearly 700 scientific institutions, 70 museums, and about 80 institutions of higher learning. The University of Moscow has more than 30,000 students. There are also hundreds of libraries.

The Cathedral of St. Sophia was destroyed by heavy fighting in World War II and had to be rebuilt after the war.

Kiev, Mother of Russian Cities

You would think that Kiev, the ancient capital of Russia, the "mother of Russian cities," would be full of glorious cathedrals and monuments dating back to the eleventh and twelveth centuries. This is only partly true.

Kiev, the present day capital of the independent republic of Ukraine, is the third largest city in the Commonwealth of Independent States behind Moscow and St. Petersburg. It was established on the Dnieper River in the ninth century and became the Russian center for the Greek Orthodox religion. The Cathedral of St. Sophia was built in the eleventh century. This magnificent building was followed by many others, including churches, monasteries, and **catacombs**.

Tragically, many of these buildings were destroyed by war. When Kiev was occupied by German armies in World War I, much damage occurred. After the Bolsheviks took over in 1917, many of the churches were converted into museums, schools, rest homes, and hospitals. Kiev was captured again by the Germans in World War II. There was much heavy fighting in what turned out to be a Soviet military disaster, and this time most of these ancient buildings, including the Cathedral of St. Sophia, were completely destroyed. St. Sophia, like many other landmark buildings, was rebuilt,

Icons are beautiful examples of Russian artwork from the Middle Ages.

but many valuable church artifacts were lost forever or stolen by the Germans.

As the cultural center of the Ukraine, Kiev has the State University of Kiev, an academy of sciences, museums, an opera house, and many libraries. Of course, all cities of any size have a share of the vast number of cathedrals, museums, libraries, historical sites, universities and scientific organizations to be found in the Commonwealth.

A Religious Background

Do you wonder why the Commonwealth has so many great churches and museums within its borders? They are the legacy of a thousand years of history. Vladimir, a grand prince of ancient Kiev, was **converted** to Christianity in 986. From that event developed the Russian Orthodox church, which eventually became a major part of the religious world. Many of the grand princes and tsars to follow Vladimir were deeply religious, as were the Russian people. Thus, many churches and cathedrals were built in Russia over the centuries.

As an example of the religious nature of the Russians and their tsars, consider the daily schedule of seventeenth century Tsar Alexis. Alexis woke up every day at 4 a.m. and went to the chapel next to his bedroom for 20 minutes of prayers. After he kissed the **icons** (religious objects) and was sprinkled with holy water, he met his wife and they went together to another chapel where they heard morning prayers and early Mass. After a couple of hours of meeting with his government officials, Tsar Alexis attended a two-hour Mass, beginning at 9 a.m. On fast days (days on which he would eat little or nothing), Alexis would attend midnight prayers for up to six hours, during which he would bow to the ground from 1,000 to 1,500 times. Tsar Alexis was an unusual case of religious fervor, but almost all of the tsars worshiped. Much of court life revolved around the observation of religious events.

THE ARTS AND SCIENCES

R E V I E W

Directions:
Number your paper from 1 to 5. Answer the following questions.
1. What makes St. Petersburg the center of Russian culture?
2. What sights could you visit if you went to the Kremlin? List four.
3. Name two things you could view if you were visiting Red Square?
4. Why are there so many churches and cathedrals in the Commonwealth?
5. What does the large number of libraries in the Commonwealth say to you?

PART 4:
Science and Space

Have you ever heard of Pavlov's dog? Pavlov refers to Ivan Petrovich Pavlov (1849-1936), the first Russian to win the Nobel Prize.

Pavlov tested the reaction of animals to certain things. He would ring a bell just before feeding a dog. After a short period of such ringing and feeding, the dog learned to associate the bell with food. When the bell rang, the dog would salivate, or drool. This meant that the dog had learned that feeding followed the ringing of the bell.

The dog's hungry reaction to the bell is called **conditioned reflex**. Pavlov's experiments led to greater understanding of how animal and human brains work. It also helped Pavlov and others to understand mental breakdown in humans.

The Academy of Sciences

Pavlov is just one of many great scientists Russia has produced. This dates back to the founding of the Academy of Sciences in St. Petersburg in 1724 by Peter the Great. The academy is the highest scientific society in Russia. It is the leader in research in the natural and social sciences, technology, and production. If there is a problem that has to be studied, researched, and solved, whether it be mental disorders, acid rain, or alcoholism, the government will turn to the academy for help.

The academy is composed of outstanding Russian and foreign scientists and scholars who gain admission only by election. The academy also trains students and publicizes important scientific achievements. In addition, it directs **research** at about 300 scientific academies and universities.

Mikhail Vasilyevi Lomonosov (lah mah NOH sav) (1711-1765) was the first great Russian scientist. He contributed to many branches of science. He was also a poet whose works are still enjoyed today in Russia, where poetry is widely read. The Academy of Science's highest award is the Lomonosov Medal.

There have been many great Russian scientists since Lomonosov. Numerous Nobel Prizes have been awarded to Russian scientists, especially in the fields of physics and chemistry.

In the Soviet Union, scientists were members of a **pampered** group. They were well-paid and received many privileges not accorded to the ordinary citizen. Much money was spent on research and equipment in many fields.

Highly trained scientists sought solutions to such problems as the use of atomic-powered icebreakers, the transmission of power over long distances, the replacement of lost or damaged limbs and organs, and the development of crops that could be grown in harsh **climates**. They also studied and researched all kinds of computer applications.

With the breakup of the Soviet Union, many of these advantages have disappeared because of a lack of money. Most scientific research has become a luxury the country cannot afford.

The Soviets in Space

Science in the former Soviet Union reached its greatest peak with the exploration of space. On October 4, 1957, the world was stunned by the announcement that the Soviet Union had launched a **sputnik** (which means **satellite**, or traveling companion). *Sputnik I* circled the Earth every 90 minutes, about 600 miles from Earth.

The Soviet achievement was so powerful and unexpected that it had serious consequences in the United States. Americans were shocked and asked why their government had allowed the Soviet Union to get so far ahead of it. Many questioned whether *Sputnik I* would eventually result in Soviet domination of the world. American educational

The Economic Achievement Center Space Museum in Moscow has many interesting displays about space exploration.

Modern Russian Architecture

Modern Russian **architecture** reflects the needs of the country for housing. Huge apartment buildings are mass-produced. They are plain and solid, with no outstanding features.

New office buildings reflect American and European styles, with a heavy emphasis on glass and marble. This is much different from the Russian architecture of old, which featured rounded domes and ornate exteriors.

institutions came under attack for not producing more scientists and engineers. There was a massive movement by students into the sciences when the public realized the military and communications value of space vehicles.

Now, many satellites circle the Earth. All are descendants of *Sputnik I.* Communications satellites bring, among other things, entertainment programs, sports, and news to your television set. Weather satellites send information and pictures back to Earth from all parts of the world, to help forecasters determine the weather in your area. Navigation satellites send back information that helps ships and planes to find their way with a high degree of accuracy. Scientific satellites are constantly probing space for answers to thousands of questions. A satellite, for instance, discovered that the Earth is not perfectly round. It is somewhat pear-shaped.

And of course there are the spy satellites launched by the former Soviet Union and by the United States. These satellites take photos of activities and structures inside both countries. The pictures are sent back to Earth and studied by national security agencies who are looking for threats to national security. A missile silo, for instance, can be detected by a satellite. Ships at sea, troop movements, and large concentrations of military equipment can also be found and photographed.

The First Man in Space

Space actually begins about 100 miles above the Earth, where the atmosphere, or air, thins to almost nothing. Space has always been a fearsome and dangerous mystery to humans. The Soviet Union was the first nation to meet the challenge of sending a man into space.

In 1957, the Soviets sent Laika, a somewhat surprised and puzzled dog, into space and brought the animal back safely. On April 12, 1961, **cosmonaut** Yuri Gagarin became the first human to travel into space when he made a single orbit around the Earth in *Vostok 1.*

For his one hour-and-48-minute ride, Gagarin became an instant Russian hero in a country devoted to its heroes.

Less than a month after Gagarin's trip, the United States sent its first man into space. Astronaut Alan Shepard went up for a 15-minute ride in *Freedom 7* (Mercury 4) but did not orbit the Earth. In February of 1962, Astronaut John Glenn became the first American to orbit the Earth, in *Friendship 7* (Mercury 6).

The Soviets edged the United States out of yet another space first in March of 1965 when Aleksei A. Leonov took the first "walk" in space. Attached to his spacecraft by a 16-foot line, Leonov spent 10 minutes floating in space.

From there, the space race was on in earnest, for military advantage and national pride. The Russians made the first landing on the Moon in January of 1966, but it was with an unmanned spacecraft. The exciting race continued when the United States put a lander on the Moon to analyze the soil, and sent back more than 10,000 photographs of the Moon's surface. On July 20, 1969, Neil Armstrong became the first man to reach the Moon's surface when he stepped down from the lunar module of his spacecraft, *Apollo 11.*

Both countries worked on space stations where crews would live for months at a time. The Soviets launched space station *Mir* in early 1987. *Mir* was designed to become the center of a large, permanently staffed space research complex. Two of its crew spent a record 366 days in space.

Incredibly, two countries that were constantly opposing each other on Earth decided to cooperate in space. In July 1975, the Soviets sent *Soyuz 19* into space and the U. S. sent *Apollo 18.* The two spacecraft met and joined together 140 miles above the Earth, where several joint experiments were conducted.

Unfortunately, political turmoil in the Soviet Union and its gradual disintegration as a country have practically put an end to Russian exploration of space for now. In 1991, three Russian cosmonauts were actually stranded in space for several months because of the political turmoil and a lack of funds.

R E V I E W

Directions:
Number your paper from 1 to 5. Answer the following questions.
1. Describe Pavlov's conditioned reflex experiments.
2. What is the function of the Russian Academy of Sciences?
3. List three Russian "firsts" in the exploration of space.
4. Who was the first man on the Moon?
5. What factors have brought the Russian space program almost to a standstill?

THE ARTS AND SCIENCES

MAP SKILLS

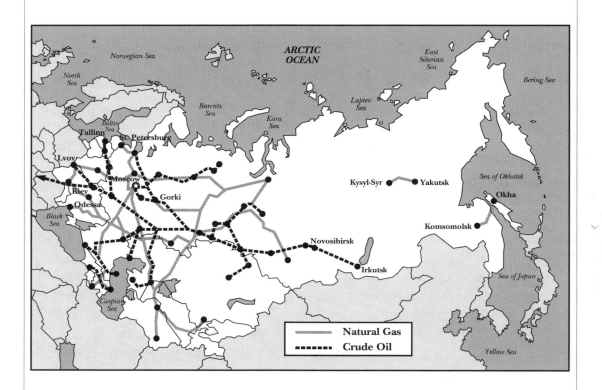

OIL AND GAS PIPELINES OF THE FORMER SOVIET UNION

Directions:

Number your paper from 1 to 10. Use the map on this page to help you answer the following questions.

1. What kind of pipeline runs through the eastern part of the former Soviet Union?

2. What kind of pipeline runs through Kiev?

3. What kind of pipeline runs between Novosibirsk and Irkutsk?

4. What kind of pipeline runs between St. Petersburg and Gorki?

5. What kind of pipeline runs between St. Petersburg and Moscow?

6. What kind of pipeline runs through Odessa?

7. What kind of pipeline can be found the farthest south?

8. How many pipelines run to cities along the Caspian Sea?

9. How many of these pipelines carry natural gas?

10. How many of these pipelines carry crude oil?

CHAPTER 4 REVIEW

Summary of the Arts and Sciences

Great Russian music continues to be played and loved throughout the world. Russian literature, like its music, reflects a deep love and concern for the country.

Russian theater and film have been a cutting edge for change, even though they were regulated by the Soviet government. Film is the most popular art form in Russia. There are more than 60,000 movie theaters in the country. Ballet is also popular and has been developed to a high degree by Russian dancers.

Russian art tends toward the historic and heroic. Marc Chagall was a leading Russian artist.

Russians love history, and this love is reflected in the creation of hundreds of museums throughout the country. St. Petersburg, Moscow, and Kiev are special centers of ancient Russian culture.

Russia has produced many great scientists. The Academy of Sciences in St. Petersburg is one of the foremost research institutions in the world.

Russian science reached a major milestone in 1957 when it launched Sputnik I. *The country also sent the first man into space.*

Critical Thinking Skills:

Directions: Give some serious thought to the questions below. Be sure to answer in complete sentences.

1. Why were Pavlov's experiments so important?
2. What role does the Academy of Sciences in St. Petersburg play in Russian life?
3. Why do you think Russian literature is still widely read and studied all over the world today?
4. Do you think the United States would have developed a space program if it had not been challenged by the Soviet Union? Explain your answer.
5. What factors have slowed down the progress of the Russian space program?

For Discussion

Directions: Discuss the following questions with your class. Appoint one class member to write the ideas you discover on the board.

1. Of the three most important cities in the C.I.S.—St. Petersburg, Kiev, and Moscow— which one would you like to visit the most? Why?
2. What do you think the large number of museums in Russia says about Russian culture?
3. How important was it for the United States to become the first country to put a man on the Moon?
4. Do you think that exploring space was worth the amount of money the former Soviet Union and the United States have spent?

Draw It!

Directions: Using information in the text and other sources, make a map of the Kremlin. Mark the locations mentioned in the text plus others you feel are important.

For You to Do

Directions: Russian author Boris Pasternak wrote a dramatic book about the Russian Civil War. Its title is *Dr. Zhivago*. A movie based on the book was made in the 1960s and is still shown on television. It is also available in video stores. Together as a class, watch the movie over several periods and discuss its portrayal of Russian culture. Could this same story be applied to other countries and another time?

GOVERNMENT

F
A
C
T
S

- All the former Soviet republics are starting from the ground up when it comes to democratic institutions.
- U.S. specialists in democratic institutions are helping the Russians revise their government structure.
- All property of the Communist party was taken from it after the party's attempted takeover of power in August 1991.
- In the first six months after the 1991 breakup of the Soviet Union, crime in Russia was up 30 percent over the previous year.

PART 1:
What Is the C.I.S.?

The Commonwealth of Independent States is not a "government" in any sense of the word. It is little more than an agreement among 11 of the 15 former Soviet republics to work together for the common good. In that, it has some similarity to the United Nations, which was formed in 1945 following World War II. The structures of the two bodies are quite different, but both serve as a way for nations to talk to one another and settle their differences without going to war.

It took many years for the United Nations to mature into an effective force for world peace. The Commonwealth in

Marx wrote that "Religion is the opiate [drug] of the masses." He believed that the ruling class invented religion to make people submissive (obedient and peaceful). Instead of questioning the social order in this world, the people would be more concerned with heaven, according to Marx.

1992 was just starting out, and even its continued existence was in doubt as the year wore on.

Some Shaky First Steps

Headquarters of the C.I.S. is in Minsk, capital of Belarus, where an administrative staff works to coordinate the activities of the 11 member republics. The core of the C.I.S. is the council of presidents of the 11 republics. They are the ones who are supposed to make the C.I.S. work.

The presidents meet several times a year to work on mutual problems. A typical list would involve trade, the military, and economic and environmental problems. An example of what the presidents talked about in a March 1992 meeting included:

- The war between Armenia and Azerbaijan.
- Ethnic violence in Moldova.
- A common military budget. (The Commonwealth armed forces have been entirely funded by Russia. Azerbaijan, Moldova, and the Ukraine were forming their own armies and didn't want to put up money for a Commonwealth army. The other republics haven't contributed anything.)
- The disposition of nuclear arms. (Eventually, the four republics that had nuclear arms on their territory—the Ukraine, Russia, Belarus and Kazakhstan—agreed to send them to Russia for safe-keeping or destruction. The handling of nuclear arms has been a major concern of the Western powers now that the central authority of the Soviet Union is no more.)
- A cooperative economic policy. (There was little agreement at the March meeting, and some members complained that if this was the way

the Commonwealth was going to operate, then it was doomed. But many had predicted the early death of the United Nations in its formative years, and in 1992 the United Nations was stronger than ever.)

The Writings of Marx

To understand the situation in the former Soviet Union today, you have to understand something of the writings of Karl Marx (1818-1883) and the world into which he was born. From there, you have to understand something of the communist state that developed from his writings, and how the Communists maintained their rigid control over the people of the Soviet Union. Then you can understand why the republics of the former Soviet Union were in such turmoil in 1992.

Marx was a social **philosopher**. He thought and wrote a lot about how people should live and how they should be governed. Marx was a German and never lived in Russia, but his thoughts and writing had their greatest effect there.

Europe of the nineteenth century was ruled by **monarchs** —kings, queens, and **tsars**. The idea of democracy, where people would rule through their elected representatives, was gaining rapidly, spurred on by the great American experiment that proclaimed rule by the people. However, many of the monarchs were still powerful, especially the Russian tsars.

Supporting these monarchs were the upper classes—landowners, industrialists, and others with money and class standing. These monarchs were also usually supported by the church. In return for its support, the church received special privileges, like low — or no — taxes.

The lower classes of Europe, the workers, had little education and lived in poverty. Although they did the work and produced the wealth, and sometimes fought and died for the upper classes, the workers got little in return. They had no hope of improving their lot under the rigid class system then in force.

Marx thought this was wrong. He thought the working man should share

People shop for colorful clothes at a market in the Ukrainian city of Lvov.

in the wealth he was producing. Marx and another German philosopher named Friedrich Engels wrote a book called *Communist Manifesto*. In it, the authors said that the bosses, or upper classes, had made slaves of the working class. Marx and Engels urged the workers to "throw off your chains" and revolt against the masters. Later, the motto of the Communist party was "Workers of All Countries, Unite!"

Marx wrote another famous book, *Das Kapital*, in which he said all history was determined by economic conditions. He offered a **theory** that he said would

Russian humor was often directed at the Soviet bureaucracy. This cartoon from Krokodil *(Crocodile), the Russian humor magazine, shows three workers laying a sidewalk. The first worker is carefully laying a cement block, while a second worker carries the blocks to him. A few feet away, a third worker is digging up the freshly laid blocks for the second worker to carry to the front of the project.*

be fair to everyone and would some day create a perfect society.

He said that the people should set up an economy in which all production would be closely planned. He said the state should own all property and all means of production. Eventually, the state would just wither away because it wouldn't be needed. All people would receive according to their needs, social classes would be erased, and everyone would then live in peace and harmony. In other words, Marx said to spread the wealth, and everything would be all right.

When Lenin and the Bolshevik (later Communist) party took over the Russian government in 1917, they did just as Marx suggested. They seized all property and means of production for the state and instituted a **planned economy**.

That was where the similarity with Marxist theory ended, however. Far from working toward a perfect society and the withering away of the state, the Bolsheviks went in the opposite direction. They made the state almighty. The people became servants to the state. And a new ruling class emerged. Instead of kings and queens to enslave and sometimes murder them, they had the Communist party.

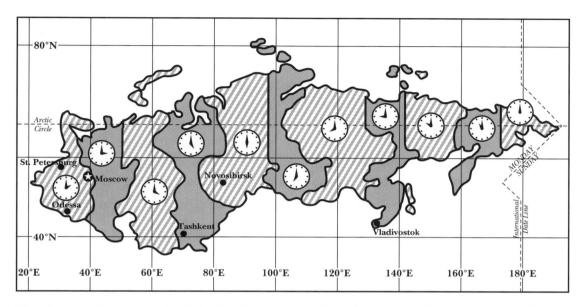

Map Study: *The former Soviet Union has 11 time zones. Name three cities on the map that are in the same time zone. If it is 2:00 in Odessa, what time will it be in Vladivostok? in Novosibirsk? in Tashkent? in Moscow? What is the time difference between Tashkent and Novosibirsk?*

The Planned Economy

Lenin and Joseph Stalin after him were rulers of the Soviet Union. Their power was as **absolute** as any monarch in the world, past or present, and they wanted a planned economy.

Thus was set up the contest between the capitalist countries, with their **market economy**, and the Soviet Union, with its planned economy. The difference between the market economy and the planned economy is at once **complex** and simple.

The United States, like most countries in the world, is a **capitalist** coun-

try. People own their own property. Factories, farms, and homes are mostly privately owned. The amount of production and the price of goods is in the hands of the people, or the market.

Suppose you are a farmer. You raise corn, tomatoes, cabbage, and beans. You sell these vegetables at a roadside stand. One year you sell a lot of corn and tomatoes, but little cabbage and beans. The market is telling you something. Corn and tomatoes are selling, but cabbage and beans are not. What does a smart farmer do? He raises the price on corn and tomatoes and drops the price on cabbage and beans to get rid of them. The next year, he grows more corn and tomatoes, and less cabbage and beans.

Under the planned economy in the former Soviet Union, a government agency, after much thought, **research**, study, and discussion, decided how much each factory, farm, and industry must produce. An agency also set prices to be charged for the goods that were produced.

Too Many Shoes

The Soviet economy worked generally on a series of plans to be accomplished in varying lengths of time. There was the dominant five-year plan; there were also annual plans, and even weekly and daily plans.

Let's say that the Heroic Shoe Factory in southern Belarus had to plan its production for the year ahead and submit it for approval to the agency responsible for shoe planning. The shoe factory management had to estimate how many shoes it could make, what kind, how much leather it would need, how many workers would be needed, what new machines would be needed, and so on. The government agency could approve the plan or change it. In any case, the agency had to figure out where the leather was coming from, where the new machinery would be built, how the goods would be transported to the shoe factory, and so on. These **calculations** went on for all means of production and involved millions of bureaucrats.

If there was a miscalculation somewhere along the line, Russians could have been up to their necks in left-footed shoes before the whole process was halted and changed. Or someone might have realized that most people wear socks with their shoes, and someone else forgot to put together a plan to supply socks to go with the mountain of shoes.

In a capitalist economy, problems can frequently be solved as simply as someone picking up the phone and saying, "How much leather have you got, how much is it, and when can I have it?" No government agency or bureaucrat is involved. And if one kind of shoe isn't selling, the company just puts it on sale to get rid of it and tries something else.

There is a danger to the individual in a capitalist — or market — economy that wasn't present in the controlled Soviet economy. If the goods made by a capitalist company aren't selling, or if the company is poorly managed, it could go broke and you could lose your job. In the former Soviet Union, no company ever went broke and few people lost their jobs, no matter how poorly they performed. The government just simply made up the losses.

Now Russia and the other former Soviet republics are trying to switch to a market economy. In 1992, the going was very difficult. The average Russian citizen didn't know what to make of a market economy and felt threatened and insecure because the market economy demands more of the worker. Also, handouts from the Soviet government used to keep prices low. Those handouts are no longer available, and prices have risen rapidly as the market economy takes hold.

R E V I E W

Directions:
Number your paper from 1 to 5. Answer the following questions.
1. Describe the class system of nineteenth century Europe.
2. What did Marx and Engels urge workers to do in their book, *Communist Manifesto?*
3. Who set the prices for goods in the former Soviet Union? What sets the prices now?
4. What is the difference between a planned economy and a market economy?
5. What has been one result of a change to the market economy in Russia?

PART 2:
Long Way to Go

To understand how far the former republics of the Soviet Union have to go to achieve democracy, you have to understand how they were governed by the Communist party.

The Soviet Union, until its breakup in 1991, was a federal republic of 15 republics, all now independent of one another. The United States is a federal republic of the 50 states.

The individual American states have wide powers over education, housing, local finances, taxes, local courts, and so on. The federal government controls national defense, foreign affairs, **commerce** between the states, and currency, among other things. The states and the United States government share certain powers, like taxation, road and bridge building, and equal rights enforcement.

In the Soviet Union, there was no true partnership between the central government and the republics. Decisions by the Communist party were simply passed down to the republics.

One-Party Government

Until 1989, it was difficult to know where the Communist party ended and the Soviet government began, as the two were so mixed up together. The top man in the Soviet Union, for instance, was not a president or a prime minister, but the general secretary of the Communist party.

Article 6 of the Soviet **constitution** established the Communist party as "the leading and guiding force" of Soviet society and the center of the political system. It was the only party permitted in the Soviet Union. When Article 6 was eliminated from the Soviet constitution in 1990, it was the first stab wound in the aging Communist giant, and eventually led to its death.

The United States has a two-party system. The major parties are the Democrats and the Republicans. Other parties are permitted, but they rarely have the voting strength to get their candidates elected.

The United States works on a system of **checks and balances** among the three branches of government. There is the legislative branch (Congress), the executive branch (the president), and the judicial branch (the federal courts).

Only twice since 1948 has one party dominated both houses of the U.S. Congress and held the presidency of the

---

Warsaw Pact

The once-mighty Warsaw Pact, a symbol of the cold war and Soviet domination of Eastern Europe, slipped into history on April 1, 1991.

The pact once bound the communist countries of East Germany, Poland, Czechoslovakia, Romania, Hungary, and Bulgaria to the Soviet Union.

The Warsaw Pact was essentially a military organization that was based on an agreement among the members to come to one another's aid in case of attack. The pact was bolstered by thousands of Soviet troops stationed on the soil of the member countries.

United States at the same time. For instance, in 1989, Republican George Bush became president. Both the U.S. House of Representatives and the U.S. Senate were controlled by the Democrats. (This means there were more Democrats than Republicans in the two houses of Congress).

President Bush and the Congress had to get along and work out their differences if anything was to get done. One branch of government cannot overwhelm the other two branches and do as it pleases with the government of the United States. This is part of the system of checks and balances.

Constitutional Government

Like the United States, the 15 independent republics of the former Soviet Union each have a constitution. So did the Soviet Union during its existence. A constitution is a basic document of any country. It is there to keep order and continuity, and to protect the rights of its citizens. A constitution is like the foundation of a house. It describes the structure of government, the way its officials are to be elected, the role of each branch of government, and the way the constitution may be changed. Most countries have a written constitution. An exception is Great Britain, whose citizens depend on tradition and the law to protect them.

The United States takes its constitution very seriously. When laws are proposed to the U.S. Congress, one of the first questions asked is whether they are

U.S. President George Bush and Soviet leader Mikhail Gorbachev hold a joint press conference after their summit meeting at Yalta in 1989. The Bush administration watched the changes going on in Eastern Europe and the Soviet Union closely. President Bush offered encouragement by sharing Gorbachev's desire for arms reduction.

constitutional. If necessary, the U.S. Supreme Court will make a ruling on the legality of particular legislation if it is brought before that body. If a law is declared unconstitutional, then it must be thrown out.

R
E
V
I
E
W

Directions:
Number your paper from 1 to 3. Answer the following questions.
1. List a similarity and a difference in the governments of the United States and the former Soviet Union.
2. What is the basic difference between a one-party system and a two-party system?
3. What was the difference in the approach of the United States and the former Soviet Union toward their constitutions?

GOVERNMENT

SPOTLIGHT
S T O R Y

Challenge in Eastern Europe

After World War II, the Soviet Union under dictator Joseph Stalin forced communist government on several countries in Eastern Europe, most of them on Russia's western borders. They were Poland, Czechoslovakia, Romania, Bulgaria, Yugoslavia, Hungary, Albania, and the German Democratic Republic, or East Germany. Any protest against communist rule in those countries was crushed by military force, as in East Berlin in 1953, Hungary in 1956, and Czechoslovakia in 1968.

In 1961, a wall was erected between East and West Berlin to keep people from escaping to the West. The Berlin Wall became a symbol of the division between the communist and capitalist countries of Europe. Hundreds of people were killed by mines or gunfire while trying to go over or through the wall to West Berlin and freedom.

In 1980, some labor leaders in Poland, under the leadership of a shipyard electrician, Lech Walesa, began to agitate against Poland's

Czechoslovakian students place posters in the window of a shop in Prague supporting the pro-democracy movement.

communist government. The movement became known as **Solidarity**. By 1989, the communist government had been forced out of office and a democratic government was in place. It was the first major, courageous step against the Communist hold on Eastern Europe.

Underlying the sudden astonishing change was a switch in the Soviet Union's attitude. No longer was it to be a restraining force, with the threat of tanks and guns behind it. The changes that had been begun by Soviet President Mikhail Gorbachev in 1985 were bearing the fruit of freedom for many countries. Gorbachev even supported the move toward self-determination.

The end of the threat of force resulted in communist governments falling one by one in 1989. Even tiny Albania, the most rigidly controlled of all communist states, overthrew its communist government in 1990.

The most important change was the sudden reunion of West and East Germany, separate countries since World War II. West Germany prospered as a democratic country while East Germany suffered under communism. The infamous Berlin Wall kept the two countries apart until it came down amid joyous celebration in late 1989.

In June of 1990, the East German parliament struck down its communist chains by eliminating the word "socialism" from its constitution and voting to turn 7,500 government businesses over to private ownership. On October 2, 1990, the two countries became one country of 75 million people. This was not without its price. The East German economy was so rundown and its people so poor that the new unified Germany was committed to spend billions of dollars to clean up the environment and create jobs for the people.

Unification worked both ways in the chaos of post-communist Europe. Czechoslovakia, created after World War I, broke apart on ethnic lines between the Czechs and Slovaks in 1992 after throwing off Communist rule.

The collapse of communism in these countries created special problems for the Soviet Union because the countries demanded that Russian troops be removed from their soil. Hundreds of thousands of troops had been stationed in these countries since World War II and now that they were being evicted, Russia had no place to put them. Tent cities were being built while housing was being constructed for the returning troops, and jobs had to be found for them. There were more than 70,000 Russian troops in Czechoslovakia alone, and 50,000 in Hungary. The last trainloads of Russian troops left those two countries in June of 1990, and many thousands from other former communist countries were soon to follow.

Violence came with the changes. In Romania, thousands of people were killed in 1989 in a bloody rebellion against the Communist leadership led by President Nicolae Ceauşescu. Ceauşescu, who was in the process of tearing down all the country villages and relocating their inhabitants into central apartments, had clearly lost his grip on reality. He and his wife were dragged from their palace, tried by a people's court, and executed in a field.

The most tragic fighting occurred in Yugoslavia. That country was sharply divided along ethnic lines but had been held together by Communist force and political skill for more than 45 years. It was an unnatural union. The six Yugoslav republics had two alphabets, three major religions, four official languages, and five major nationalities.

Croatia and Slovenia broke the republic apart in June of 1991 when they declared their independence from Yugoslav rule. Serbia, also a part of the communist state of Yugoslavia, sought to expand its territory at the expense of its former sister republics in a series of complicated events. Fighting broke out as Serbian troops moved against Croatia and later Bosnia-Herzegovina. Fighting was especially bitter in Bosnia, where the Serbians tried to cleanse certain parts of Bosnia of their Muslim population.

Terrible atrocities were committed by all sides and it was estimated that more than 100,000 people had died in battle or from hunger by late 1992. The European powers, fearful that the fighting would spread to other countries as the nationalities tried to settle their ethnic differences with warfare, were unable to bring peace to the region by negotiation. By late 1992, United Nations peacekeepers were in place to bring food and medical supplies to civilians in the war zones.

Stop and Review

Answer these questions in your own words.

1. What Soviet dictator forced the communist system of government on nearby countries?

2. How did the Soviet Union respond to protest against Communist rule in nearby countries in the 1950s and 1968?

3. What did the Berlin Wall represent after it was erected in 1961?

4. What two countries unified in 1990? What was the population of the unified country?

5. In what two countries has there been bitter fighting in recent years?

GOVERNMENT

PART 3:
A New Government

Change came so rapidly to the republics of the former Soviet Union that there was little time to develop a government structure to meet the needs of democracy.

The Communist party and the Soviet government were tightly **structured** units with highly disciplined bureaucrats who ran the day-to-day operations with

A war veteran wearing his medals is a common sight in the former Soviet Union.

a strong hand. In 1992, Boris Yeltsin, as president, and the Russian parliament were the two major instruments of power in Russia.

The parliament is made up of two bodies: the **Congress of People's Deputies** and the **Supreme Soviet**. The Supreme Soviet has about 200 members who are elected by the Congress of People's Deputies from its own 1,000-member body. The Supreme Soviet handles the day-to-day legislative work and proposed laws to the Congress of People's Deputies, which has been meeting twice a year.

Russian president Boris Yeltsin was the major political force, with vast powers to run the country by **edict**. That is, he could personally issue an order with the force of law and people were supposed to obey it. Thus, he frequently bypassed his own parliament. The Congress of People's Deputies in 1992 was made up mainly of former Communists who wanted to return to the old ways, and its members were constantly opposing Yeltsin's programs.

Government varied from republic to republic in the former Soviet Union in 1992. The Baltic states, with a history of

A young Russian soldier in St. Petersburg.

Major Points of C.I.S. Agreement

- The Commonwealth of Independent States would not in itself be a state, but an alliance of fully independent states. Commonwealth policy would be set through a council made up of the presidents of member republics.
- The individual states would assume ownership of the national government (the former Soviet Union) civilian facilities on their soil.
- Russia, the Ukraine, and Belarus would retain their memberships in the United Nations, with Russia taking over the Soviet Union's seat on the Security Council. The other states would seek seats in the U.N.
- The Commonwealth would honor the Soviet Union's arms control agreements. (A Soviet army general was appointed to command all Soviet armed forces pending discussions on a Commonwealth military structure. Later, it became obvious that each republic wanted to hold onto its slice of the military pie, and some republics moved toward forming their own military force. There was also an argument between Russia and the Ukraine over control of the powerful Black Sea fleet of 300 warships. The two countries eventually put off a decision until 1995 on how to split up the fleet.)

managing their own affairs, had well-structured legislative and executive branches. In fact, the Baltic States were democratic well before the breakup of the Soviet Union. Some of the poorer southern republics, generally isolated from the other former Soviet republics, still leaned on the old, rigid Communist structure for government. Many former Communists were in control in those republics, and democracy was making little progress.

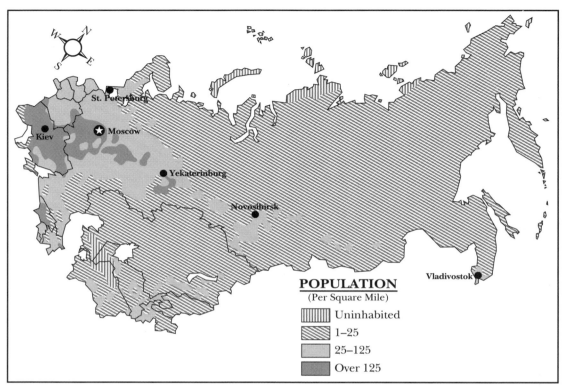

POPULATION
(Per Square Mile)

▓ Uninhabited
▓ 1–25
▓ 25–125
▓ Over 125

Map Study: *What is the population per square mile in Novosibirsk? in Yekaterinburg? in Moscow? Is the C.I.S. more heavily populated in the western or eastern republics? Name one part of the former Soviet Union (north, south, east, or west) that is uninhabited.*

In 1992, there was no way to predict the course of the shaky democratic movement and the future structure of government in many of the former republics.

Voting Rights

In March of 1989, the first free elections were held to fill the then 2,250-seat Congress of People's Deputies, with startling results.

To understand why the results were startling, you have to know something about the way elections were held by the Communist party from 1917 to 1989. The United States and the former Soviet Union had similar election laws. Everyone 18 years old or older could vote. There were no educational, literacy, or religious restrictions.

The Soviet people were encouraged

to vote, and about 99 percent of those eligible usually did. (The United States average in national elections is much lower. In the 1992 presidential election, about 55 percent of the electorate voted.)

Until 1989, when voters in the Soviet Union went to vote, they found only one name on the ballot for each office. All voters could do was vote "Yes" or "No." The candidate on the ballot was selected by the Communist party or by trade unions, farmers cooperatives, and factory organizations, all under the leadership of the party. Naturally, the party choice always won by a huge margin.

In March 1989, Soviet voters went to the polls to elect members of the Congress of People's Deputies by secret ballot, giving the voter a choice for the first time in 72 years. Not all candidates were party members, and in fact many Communist candidates actually lost. Among the big winners was Boris Yeltsin, running for a seat in the Congress. Of the 6.8 million registered voters, 5.1 million voted for him and only 400,000 for his Communist opponent. This election revealed deep dissatisfaction with the way the Communist party was running the country, and it was Yeltsin's first step toward supreme power in Russia.

A young man with jeans and a Western-style haircut reflects a growing interest in Western fashions and attitudes among young people in the C.I.S. The sight of Western clothing is also evidence of a thriving black market, an illegal network of buying and selling goods. Some black market activities are tolerated by officials, but those marketeers who are prosecuted can face long prison terms.

Gone With the Wind

All the old Communist structures have been swept away in Russia and in many of the other independent republics, and the republics are struggling with ways to replace them with democratic organizations. The Communist party, once with 20 million highly privileged members, is no longer a political force. Collective farms still exist, but their days are numbered as Russia moves to a private economy.

Such basic Communist staples as the **Komsomol**, which prepared Russian youth for membership in the party, the **Young Octoberists**, and the **Young Pioneers**, all Communist organizations to control youthful thinking and activities, are mostly gone. Some remnants remain, but their days too are numbered.

Another foundation of Soviet and Communist power was the military. The military power is still there because of its sheer size, but now the parts are fragmented, the equipment is in poor repair, and the huge money outlays for weapons are no longer there. The military is not even sure what its role is anymore, and the larger republics are in the process of creating their own armies.

Another institution that was rigidly controlled by the Communist party was the court system. The courts existed to serve the political needs of the Communist party and had little to do with justice, except at the lowest levels.

Russia has created a Constitutional Court to deal with matters of a high level, but its role is still unclear. Some compare it to the U.S. Supreme Court, oth-

---

Tips for the Russians

While some Americans take a dim view of how their government works, others in the world would be happy to be dealing with the federal **bureaucracy** of the United States.

For two weeks in 1992, the governments of Russia and Kazakhstan were host to a visiting delegation of U.S. government lawyers and experts on democratic government. The visitors were teaching the Russians such things as regulation-writing and resolution of disputes.

Russian delegations have come to the United States to study how our state legislatures work. Later, they will also visit Washington, D.C., to study the Congress of the United States and the way it works.

---

ers call it a test run to find out if the Russians can deal with an honest and non-political court system.

One of its first cases involved a strange suit. Thirty-seven pro-Communist legislators sued Russian President Boris Yeltsin in early 1992 over his banning of the party and the seizing of its assets. The Communists claimed these acts were illegal. The thirteen judges hearing the case are all former Communists, because until 1990 it was impossible to become a judge in the Soviet Union without being a party member. The case is expected to last for many months.

In many ways, however, certain basic legal procedures are unchanged. The People's Courts are the lowest courts. They consider cases of all kinds. Each court has one judge, elected by the voters. The judge is assisted by people who are not required to have legal training. These **people's assessors** are not paid. The move in Russian courts is toward the rule of law instead of the party.

R
E
V
I
E
W

Directions:
Number your paper from 1 to 5. Answer the following questions.
1. What is an edict?
2. What are the names of the two bodies of the Russian parliament?
3. Name three former Communist organizations that no longer exist.
4. Why are some pro-Communists suing Russian President Boris Yeltsin?
5. Do collective farms still exist?

MAP SKILLS

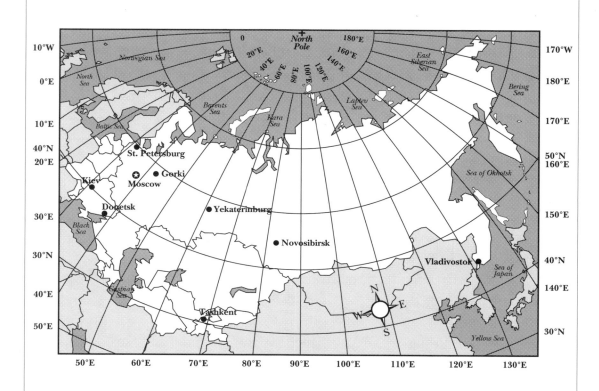

LATITUDE AND LONGITUDE

Directions: Use the map on this page to help you answer questions about longitude and latitude.

1. (Tashkent, Vladivostok) is located near 41° north latitude and 69° east longitude.

2. (St. Petersburg, Gorki) and Yekaterinburg are located near the same latitude.

3. (Donetsk, Novosibirsk) is located near 48° north latitude and 37° east longitude.

4. St. Petersburg and (Moscow, Kiev) are located near the same longitude.

5. (St. Petersburg, Yekaterinburg) is located near 57° north latitude and 61° east longitude.

6. (Gorki, Kiev) is located near 50° north latitude and 30° east longitude.

7. (Novosibirsk, Gorki) is located near 55°north latitude and 83°east longitude.

8. Vladivostok is located near ___° north latitude and ___° east longitude.

CHAPTER 5 REVIEW

Summary of Government

The Commonwealth of Independent States is not a government. It is an agreement among 11 of the 15 former Soviet republics to work together for the common good. C.I.S. headquarters is in Minsk, capital of the republic of Belarus. An administrative staff coordinates the activities of the C.I.S. republics. The Council of Presidents meets several times a year to discuss and resolve problems.

The writings of Karl Marx formed the basis of communist theory, but party leaders led the Soviet Union away from some of his basic ideas. To understand where the former Soviet republics are now, it is helpful to understand some of what Marx wrote and the world he lived in. A planned economy was one of the foundations of Communist leadership.

Many of the former Soviet republics rely on a president and a parliament to run their government. In 1992, President Boris Yeltsin was the major political force in Russia.

All of the old Communist party structures have been swept away. In their place, the newly independent republics are struggling to find acceptable organizations to replace them. The military is having problems adjusting to the new situation. The court system is being revised. But there are many things the Russians have to learn about democratic institutions.

Critical Thinking Skills

Directions: Give some serious thought to the questions below. Be sure to answer in complete sentences.

1. What was the condition of the masses in Europe that led Karl Marx to seek change in the way they were ruled? Why did he think change was necessary?

2. How does the Commonwealth of Independent States differ from what we think of as a government?

3. Why has it been difficult to build a new government to replace the old Communist government?

4. How did the U.S. government differ from the way the Soviet government worked?

5. How did the 1989 elections reveal the weakness of the Communist party?

For Discussion

Directions: Discuss these questions with your class. Appoint one class member to write the ideas you discover on the board.

1. If you had lived in the Soviet Union, would you have supported or opposed the changes that took place there? Why?

2. Why do you think a higher percentage of Russian voters than American voters go to the polls to vote?

3. How have the writings of Karl Marx affected our lives even today?

Write It!

Directions: Write a dialogue between a Russian teenager and his grandfather who lived through World War II. Have them discuss past and present changes they have seen in their government.

For You to Do

Directions: Many things important to the future of the world are going on right now. There are stories in the newspapers almost every day about changes in Eastern Europe and Russia. Each day for one month, clip stories from newspapers and magazines about Russia and Eastern Europe. Read through all the articles and keep a scrapbook. Be prepared to discuss the articles with your classmates.

LIFE TODAY

Chapter 6

- A favorite game of Russian children is "Cossacks and robbers."
- In Yakutsk in Siberia, schools don't close unless it's 58 degrees below zero.
- Many recent world chess champions have come from Russia.
- Estonia, Latvia, Lithuania, and Georgia decided not to join the C.I.S.

PART 1:
The Reality of Being Russian

" I've had television for ten years now. For nine years it served as a plant stand," said Svetlana Molseya, a middle-aged, middle-class woman in December of 1990. "Now I turn it on. There is something to watch.

"Now I believe what they show me is the real world. I see food lines, I see drug addiction, I see people from the West on our television. And I hear real discussions about our political system. This is real life, good and bad. This is exciting."

It has gotten a little less exciting for Svetlana Molseya since then. With the breakup of the Soviet Union in December of 1991 came higher prices, more crime, fewer goods, and less food. Although the struggle over press freedom and the freedom to say what you want on television continues, no one believes there will be a return to the old days of strict censorship.

The Communist party thought of television as a way to spread its message, and television sets were a priority item of production in the Soviet Union. Now the Communist party is outlawed in Russia and in some of the other republics of the Commonwealth of Independent States. But there are still plenty of former Communist party members around, many of them in important positions. For example, in 1992, 86 percent of the members of the Congress of People's Deputies, the major legislative body in Russia, were former members of the Communist party.

An example of the struggle for continued freedom of expression in Russia was the fight that developed in 1992 for control of *Izvestia,* once the voice of the Communist party but later a **liberal** daily newspaper. The leaders of the Russian parliament wanted to bring *Izvestia* under its control and dictate its editorial policies and censor its news columns. Russian president Boris Yeltsin declared such an act as "illegal" and said that *Izvestia,* and all other newspapers, would be free to print what they wanted.

The battle is much bigger than the fate of one newspaper. The winner will eventually control all methods of communication in Russia. The struggle will probably go on for years in one form or another.

Meanwhile, Russian television continues to extend its horizons, providing

What Do Russians Eat?

There is very little purely Russian food because the C.I.S. is a collection of many nationalities and customs. The basic peasant foods range from Mongolian through Turkish to Polish.

What people eat in the C.I.S. depends on other factors besides nationality. Where they live and what is available at the market also determine what they consume. Food in the southern republics is often similar to food in nearby countries such as Turkey and Greece. Lamb, sausage, chicken, and fish are frequently cooked over an open fire on skewers and are sometimes covered with nuts or cheese. In Siberia, Oriental spices add flavor to horse and reindeer meat, as well as to canned fish.

For most of the country, the main meal of the day is lunch, which is usually eaten at work. It's easier this way because of the long lines people have to stand in to buy food for the home. Children eat their big meal of the day at school.

An average meal in many Russian homes consists of cheese, sardines, maybe a potato, and the thick brown bread that Russians love. Tea is usually served with most meals.

Russians love to snack. They always seem to be munching on a small piece of this or that before and after regular meals. Perhaps this is because food can sometimes be hard to come by.

A favorite Russian dish is **borscht,** an Eastern European beet-based soup or stew that is popular in Poland and the Soviet Union. American visitors say the whole country lives on some form of borscht.

a window on the West and a view of real life in Russia and the world. The broadcasts run from soft drink commercials in English, shown during American basketball games, to rock videos, politicians in debate, and priests baptizing babies. Under strict Communist rule, the real world was hidden from view. Anything that cast a shadow on the government was not allowed.

The TV "Shock Factor"

Russian television viewers are finding it difficult to adjust to the new freedom on TV.

Dima Dyakorov, an artist, watches TV for its "shock factor." He is still amazed at some of the things that appear on the "blue screen," as TV is called in Russia. He recounts one discussion on a late-night show where a panel of people argued about the removal of Lenin from his tomb in Red Square.

"I was absolutely stunned," he said. "I thought I had not heard right. But no, they were saying 'Lenin,' not 'Stalin.' I was waiting for the speakers to be dragged off by soldiers."

TV deals with controversial subjects like AIDS, abortion, finance, and the failures of the Communist party in its role as ruler of the former Soviet Union. These themes are revolutionary, considering that until 1989 the most exciting productions on Soviet TV were a Polish dance troupe or discussions on communist thought.

Now Russians stare transfixed at the sight of Michael Jackson strutting on stage, or young women in miniskirts smiling and singing as they gulp down fizzy sugar water, or well-dressed men and women slapping down a credit card to pay for the riches they meet at every turn. None of this corresponds to reality in Russia.

The impressions can be misleading, if not confusing. One taxi driver asked a visitor from the United States, "Do you really sing when you drink Pepsi-Cola?"

Change was the word for life in Russia and the other republics of the Commonwealth of Independent States in 1992. The Soviet Union and the Com-

In the former Soviet Union, many private homes do not have telephones. Most public phones can be found in front of local post offices like this one in Kiev.

munist party no longer existed, but the damage done under their rule continues to make life difficult for the average Russian. Freedom of thought and speech is much improved, but material life for the average Russian has gone downhill.

A Typical Story

Sergei Latyshev was a foreign correspondent for a news agency for five years. He returned to Russia in 1992 to find everything had changed for the worse.

Because of the housing shortage, it is not unusual for several generations of one family to live in the same apartment.

"Strange things occur in Moscow now," he said. "There are no more jokes on the streets or in the kitchens about the way the Communists used to run things. Fruit for our nine-year-old daughter is not a problem—we just don't think about it. Getting basic meals is problem enough."

The Russian government instituted price increases in January of 1992 as the country moved into a **market economy** and away from the command economy run by the Communists.

"Prices have jumped 40 to 100 times, but my salary has stayed the same," Latyshev said. "Bread costs keep rising, and friends who used to be fat are now rather slim. The most mysterious thing happened to our **rubles**. They are gone after three weeks of living in Moscow. I thought we were set for a year."

Food shops in Moscow are disappearing because they have nothing to sell. They are being taken over by commercial shops, in which a miserable variety of soft drinks, outdated stereos, shirts, and tennis balls are being sold at outrageously high prices. Latyshev asked the price of a leather jacket in one of those shops.

"I was told it was 21,000 rubles. I am lucky to be making 1,700 rubles a month," Latyshev said. He complains about other things.

"Amid hungry pensioners begging for food you see vulgar-looking young men driving expensive cars," he said. "Everyone knows success now means you steal from the public sector, re-sell, work financial frauds, or participate in go-between operations. A friend in a reputable foreign car sales company says, 'All our clients are crooks.' "

Latyshev hopes that everything will straighten out once the turmoil ends and the Russian government gets a grip on the economy and brings back law and order. Many foreign experts believe this will take a long time, and many bad things will happen in the meantime.

A Typical Family

One typical Commonwealth family of five lives in an apartment in the Ukrainian capital city of Kiev. In 1989, Alexander Nikityuk, 81, was retired on a state **pension** of 120 rubles a month. His wife, Antonina, 75, was also retired and was given 80 rubles a month. Their daughter, Tatyana, 38, is a freelance writer but makes little money. Her husband, Victor, 41, is an engineer at a **research** center. After 14 years on the job, he is making 260 rubles a month. Victor and Tatyana have a daughter, Katya, who is eight and in the second grade.

In 1989, a ruble was worth roughly about $1.60, so the family had an income of about $736 a month. But in 1992, a comparison between Ukrainian or Russian rubles and the American dollar was almost impossible to make because of rapidly rising prices in the Commonwealth and the general disarray of the Commonwealth economic system as it made the transition to a market economy.

The Nikityuks can't afford a larger apartment and may even have to give up the one they have. The Soviet Union, when it existed, controlled apartment prices and generally kept them at a low level regardless of the size of the apartment. In 1989, the Nikityuks paid 35 rubles—$56—a month. In 1992, with the Russian leadership still trying to figure things out, controls are to be lifted and prices will rise.

Home for the five members of the Nikityuk family is three rooms crammed with bookcases and furniture. The grandfather sleeps in a small room by himself. The grandmother and granddaughter sleep in a second room. The mother and father have no bedroom for themselves. They sleep in what passes for the living room, or sometimes they switch with the other members of the family.

The Nikityuks have a strong sense of family, as most Russians do. But they wonder why they must all live in one tiny apartment. The problem is the chronic

SPOTLIGHT
S T O R Y

The Environment

Not too long ago, the Aral Sea was the fourth largest inland body of water in the world. Now it is the sixth. What happened is being pointed to as a sign of the long-term consequences of a Soviet development policy that neglected environmental concerns.

Under Communist rule, a cotton culture was developed in Uzbekistan, the largest and most populous of the former Central Asia Soviet republics. But massive **irrigation**, fertilization, and spraying programs caused major environmental damage. Much of the water used in irrigation came from the Aral Sea, and it has shrunk to half its original volume of water since the early 1960s.

Diseases caused by salt and unfiltered water have led to kidney stones in the populace, anemia, and tuberculosis. The region's fish-processing industry has shut down because the fish are dying from the sea's high salt content, causing the loss of thousands of jobs.

The meltdown of the nuclear power plant at Chernobyl in 1986 is just one of a number of major disasters brought on by Communist neglect of the **environment**.

Radioactive wastes were dumped directly into fish-filled streams and lakes. Wrecked nuclear submarines and other ships were left lying abandoned on the ocean floor. Chernobyl-style nuclear reactors were left to putter along without maintenance or oversight or the likelihood of repairs.

Such were the nuclear practices of the former Soviet Union, as detailed in a special field hearing held by the United States Senate Intelligence Committee.

Radioactive wastes from the regime once considered the greatest threat to world peace now pose an ecological threat to the Earth's entire northern region, according to U.S. scientists and government officials.

Some other threats:

- Wastes from plutonium extraction at the Soviet Union's first nuclear weapons site at Chelybinsk, in southern Siberia, were dumped directly into the Techa River, contaminating the watershed. After 1951, the Soviets switched their dumping to Lake Karachay, where today one hour's exposure at the shoreline is considered fatal by physicians.

- Nuclear weapons testing at Novaya Zemlya released a total of 300 megatons of radioactive waste into the atmosphere as far away as Alaska and northern Canada. Among the tests was a 1961 blast that was 3,000 times more powerful than the Hiroshima explosion.

- Nuclear-powered submarines and other vessels that sank after accidents or mechanical failures now threaten the marine environment. Among the vessels in the Arctic Ocean is the midsection and three nuclear reactors of the Icebreaker Lenin. The Pacific Ocean is also threatened. In 1985, for example, a nuclear submarine exploded in Vladivostok while refueling.

- Creaky Soviet-era nuclear power plants, built without safeguards, continue to pump out energy, while the financially strapped Russian government is unable to make repairs. Some 15 Chernobyl-style reactors were in operation in 1992. Cancer deaths around Siberian nuclear sites have skyrocketed over the past decades. Particularly hard hit are infants and Siberian natives. The news about Soviet nuclear pollution is alarming many Alaskans. Ocean currents, atmospheric flows, and migrating polar ice could sweep the nuclear contamination from Siberia's north coast to Alaska and arctic areas.

- The Caspian Sea, a major source of fish for food, is heavily polluted by the oil industries on its shores.

Stop and Review

Write the answers to these questions on your paper.

1. Why is the Aral Sea drying up?
2. What major industry has been shut down by the loss of water in the Aral Sea?
3. What particular kind of waste is causing alarm throughout the world?
4. What sea is heavily polluted by the oil industry?
5. Why can't the Russian government make repairs on its nuclear reactors?

housing shortage in Russia and the other Commonwealth republics. The Communist party placed military might ahead of civilian goods, and what housing they did build was poorly constructed and quickly fell into disrepair.

Now government authorities have to cope with housing the hundreds of thousands of troops returning from countries in Eastern Europe and the Baltic states, where they are no longer wanted. No one knows how that will be done.

This was the reality of life in much of the Commonwealth in 1992. It showed the difference between **glasnost**, where people can express themselves freely, and **perestroika**, or economic restructuring. Glasnost is nice, but the people would also like something to eat, some clothing to wear, and a decent place to live.

REVIEW

Directions:
Number your paper from 1 to 5. Answer the following questions.

1. Provide an example of how your family life differs from that of a Russian family.
2. What kinds of shows air on Russian television? Why does the selection of programs surprise many Russians?
3. Why is it difficult to compare the Russian ruble with the American dollar?
4. Why is there a housing shortage in the Commonwealth of Independent States?
5. How were apartment prices kept low in the former Soviet Union?

PART 2:
Change Comes to the Farm

In the 1920s and 1930s, Lenin and Stalin collectivized the farms. That is, they took the land away from its owners—the peasants—and brought it together in huge **collectives**, on which people worked for wages. The Communists thought this would be a more efficient way of producing food, and they also wanted to eliminate private ownership of land. In the United States, most farmers own their own land and sell their crops on the **market** for whatever they can get for them. When prices in the U.S. drop below a certain point set by the government, the government steps in and makes up the difference between market prices and the price set by the government. This is done to protect small farmers and keep them in business.

Under communism in the Soviet Union, the government planned everything. It told the collectives what they could plant, when they could plant, and how much they could plant. The government sold fertilizer and farm machinery to the collectives. Most of what was produced on the collectives in the Soviet Union went to the state.

However, the collective system was not able to adequately supply the needs of the population. Food shortages and even **famines** in which thousands died have been a problem since the Bolshevik Revolution. Because of the problems caused by the recent collapse of the old government structure and the shattering of the Soviet Union, food problems have gotten even worse.

The system is changing slowly from a collective farm economy to one like that of the United States, where farmers can own their own land and sell their crops for what they can get.

A major step came in March of 1990, when the Soviet **legislature** voted to give citizens the right to own land, build on it, and use it for private profit. At the time, this was a major break in the rigid Communist system.

Russians often have to wait in long lines to buy food and other goods. Sometimes they will get into a line before they know what is being sold because they figure it is probably something they will need.

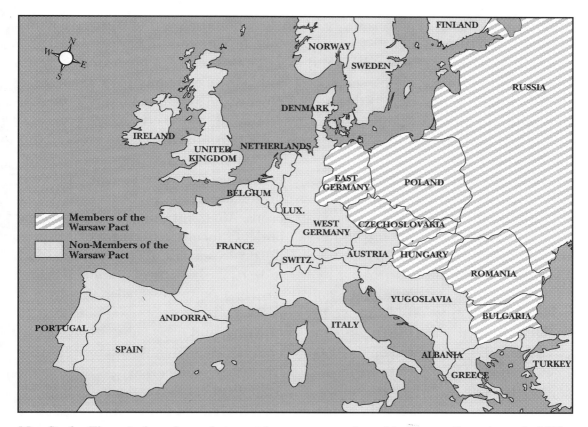

Map Study: *The map above shows what countries were once members of the Warsaw Pact prior to the 1990s. (Albania withdrew in 1968.) The Warsaw Pact was basically a military organization that was based on an agreement to come to each other's defense in case of attack. How many countries were members of the Warsaw Pact? Which member (country) of the Warsaw Pact was located the farthest south? Was Austria a member of the Warsaw Pact? East Germany? West Germany? Finland?*

Since the breakup of the Soviet Union, things have gotten even more confusing, but there is no doubt that Russian **agriculture** is moving toward a private system of ownership. The problem now is that no one has developed a really workable farm policy and the politicians who ran the collectives want to hold onto their power. These politicians, most of them hard-line Communists used to the privilege and power that went with running large collectives, make it difficult for the private farmer to obtain fertilizer and machinery and to market crops.

Russian President Boris Yeltsin has

told the peasants to obtain land, raise crops, and sell them. But in 1992 no one has told the farmers how this would work. In the meantime, people still work their little plots, and the collectives still operate under the old system.

Debate over Land

During World War II, Russian peasants began working around the rules on collectivization. The government encouraged people to grow food on plots near their towns to help feed the population. Day after day during the growing season, men too old to fight, along with women and young children, would trudge from their villages to cultivate the plots. The produce was sold on the open market and did not have to be turned over to the state.

Soon people began building small sheds to store their tools. Then they began fencing off their plots. The peasants soon started to expand their sheds, and soon the sheds grew into small cottages. They became homes in the country, or **dachas**.

Do you see what was happening? The people were taking over land that belonged to the state. They were working harder on their own plot of land than they did on the collective farms, and making the land pay off for them. This was private enterprise, the cornerstone of economic life in the Western nations that the Communist party so hated.

After the war, a bitter debate arose within the Communist party about these plots. Stalin and his followers wanted to reclaim the plots and tear down the cottages. Others began to look at the amount of food grown on these "private" plots. They discovered that the plots were producing a high percentage of Soviet crops. Amazingly, the three percent of Soviet farmland in the private plots produced 25 percent of the country's food in 1991, the last year of Communist rule.

The Communists failed to solve the problems in agriculture despite decades of trying, and their failure was a major reason the communist system eventually failed. The problems in agriculture have a ripple effect that spreads through all the republics of the Commonwealth of Independent States. A major occupation of Russian women is standing in line for hours, usually for food. Sometimes they see a line and stand in it without even knowing what is for sale.

The Problems Continue

The lack of modern equipment and spare parts, the gradual movement of labor from farms to cities, and a weak transportation system outside the major cities have combined to keep production and distribution below acceptable levels. Less than 20 percent of rural roads are paved. They are often axle-deep in mud, meaning that many crops are left in the fields to rot because they can't be distributed. Farm experts have estimated that 30 percent of all crops in the C.I.S. never get to market and are lost.

At the heart of collectivized farming was central planning. Regional officials would tell chairmen of each collective how to run the farms. Deadlines for planting and harvest had to be met regardless of the weather. This has changed in theory, but it hasn't changed in fact. Until the stranglehold of collective officials is finally broken and someone comes up with a strong farm policy, the Commonwealth will continue to have trouble feeding itself.

R E V I E W

Directions:
Number your paper from 1 to 5. Answer the following questions.
1. How did World War II affect collective farming?
2. What was the subject of a major debate in the Soviet Union after World War II?
3. Why is it so difficult to distribute farm products in the C.I.S.?
4. What changes do you think are coming to agriculture in the C.I.S.?
5. What was one of the reasons for the failure of the communist system?

LIFE TODAY

PART 3:
Music, Cars, and Religion

Western **culture** arrived in the Soviet Union well before the breakup of that country, and Communist authorities were not happy about it. They thought Western culture took the minds of the people off Soviet business.

One example of Western culture that was a big hit was a giant rock concert in Moscow which Russian musicians claimed made Moscow the "rock capital of the world" for one weekend in August of 1989. That weekend also happened to mark the twentieth anniversary of Woodstock, the famous American rock festival. For two days, 100,000 rock fans crowded into Lenin Stadium to hear bands performing in the Moscow Music Peace Festival. The profits went to

Most Russians get from one place to another by public transportation, like this streetcar in St. Petersburg.

treatment for alcoholics and drug addicts in Russia.

Heavy metal fans in their black leather and hippies in their faded jeans mingled together for two 10-hour concerts. Two electronic scoreboards listed the names of the bands: Ozzy Osbourne from Great Britain; Nuance, Brigada, and Gorky Park from the Soviet Union; Skid Row, Cinderella, Motley Crue, and Bon Jovi from the United States; and Scorpions from West Germany.

Songs About Freedom

The Russian rock fans liked Scorpions and Bon Jovi best. Rock music seems to play a different role in Russian society than it does in America. Russian rock musicians perform songs about soul, freedom, and even perestroika.

Even older citizens have been drawn to rock music, for unusual reasons. A middle-aged woman, Anastasia Vanik, told an American friend that she had attended a benefit rock concert for Armenian earthquake relief by the British rock group Pink Floyd.

"There is nothing else to do and spend rubles on," she said. "And everyone saw the concert as a symbolic **milestone** in Russian culture because it represented the freedom to do as we want."

So it goes with the Russian youth, who are rapidly becoming Westernized, especially in the big cities. The "old" Russian way was to stay on the farm, work hard, and raise a large family. This has changed with the rapid move to the cities and the decline of the birth rate. The birth rate in Russia and the other C.I.S. republics has dropped alarmingly, except in the poorer republics of Central Asia.

Teenagers in Russia now are like teenagers everywhere. They like pop music (the late Beatle John Lennon is practically a national hero), and jeans are very popular. Jeans and other articles of Western-style clothing are now being made in Russia and in Eastern European countries. Jeans have a special appeal because they represent what Russian youths view as the excitement of America. One Russian teenager was even seen wearing a T-shirt that said "I Shot J.R." (J.R. Ewing was a character in the popular American TV program "Dallas.")

One of the things that led to the downfall of the Communist structure was the loss of the younger generation. Many young people had joined the party just to stay out of trouble, but they had no interest in the party and took no part in its activities.

Fourteen Million Autos

The large cities of the Commonwealth of Independent States are a strange mixture of the old and the new. Moscow, for instance, has ancient cathedrals, churches, **museums**, and the massive walls of the Kremlin overlooking broad, modern boulevards.

Deep beneath the streets runs the fast, efficient metro, a subway system built in the 1930s. The Moscow subway is the fourth largest in the world behind New York, London, and Paris. There are 150

Worshipers file into a Ukrainian Orthodox church in Lvov.

December 1989: Soviet President Mikhail Gorbachev visits the Vatican in Rome and meets with Pope John Paul II.

miles of lines. The system's 27,000 employees send out 8,000 trains each day on nine lines. The subway is one of the few things that work well in Russia.

Why? Because if it didn't, some say, Moscow would collapse. The big blue trains are always packed. Riders have to jab and lurch their way on and off. Russia gives as much attention to its subway system as it does to its space program. Subway motormen are paid three to four times as much as factory workers and are also provided with apartments.

As one Russian official said: "Rocket plants and auto plants may close, but the subway will keep working. If the subway stops, Moscow will die." But the money crunch is even affecting this pride of Russia these days. The crazily ornate stations, with their statuary and stained glass, were usually kept spotless and the

equipment in top repair. Now spare parts are hard to come by, and the walls are no longer clean.

The subway and train systems are an important part of Russian culture because there are relatively few automobiles, and daily lives revolve around transportation schedules. There were only 14 million cars registered in the C.I.S. in 1991, compared with 190 million in the United States.

All C.I.S. cities are dominated by huge blocks of apartments. Many of them are in disrepair because of poor workmanship and neglect. There are few single-family homes in the cities.

Religion

The Russian people can now celebrate their various religions as they please after decades of harsh restrictions under the Communist leadership. This has been one of the greatest of all changes in the now democratic Commonwealth.

Russian religious culture goes back to the year 988, when some of the groups that inhabited Western Russia were converted to Christianity. For the next thousand years, a deep religious base grew. Religious groups, especially the Russian Orthodox church, became a major force in Russian culture. Thousands of churches and cathedrals were built. The

tsars promoted the idea that they themselves represented the Word of God, believing this helped to keep the peasantry in line. The tsars also used the church to support their policies.

All this changed in 1917 with the Bolshevik Revolution. The Bolsheviks were atheists—they did not believe in God. Also, they didn't want competition from the religious orders. They wanted the people to substitute the state for God. Although religion was never officially outlawed, by 1921 more than half of Russia's monasteries had been closed, countless churches had been destroyed, and many bishops and priests were arrested. Moscow's magnificent Cathedral of Christ the Savior was blown up. Other churches were converted to hospitals, museums, schools, and other uses.

Since the advent of the Commonwealth at the beginning of 1992, restrictions on religion have been swept away, but some tension exists between the various religions, particularly between Muslims and Christians in the southwestern republics.

Russian Jewry

Another great change that has occurred in Russia and the other Commonwealth republics has been the treatment of the Jewish population. Jews in Russia were harassed and persecuted by the tsars for hundreds of years. **Pogroms**, organized, official programs of violence, vandalism, and rioting that often led to murder, swept across Russia periodically during tsarist rule.

Under communism, Jews were frequently jailed, deprived of their jobs and sometimes murdered. Those who tried to leave the Soviet Union were often sent to Siberia. At the very least, they lost their jobs. Jewish intellectuals often led the fight against Communist persecution. They were thrown in prison for years or sent to insane asylums, where they were sedated with drugs.

Now the Jewish population faces no restrictions. Jews can come and go as they please, and many thousands have gone to live in Israel, where they feel safe from harassment. A great burden has been placed on the Israeli government to find these newcomers housing and jobs, and many well-educated Jews are now finding themselves fortunate to have a job sweeping the streets in Israel. Anti-Jewish feelings are still strong in Russia, and many of the Jews there feel isolated and threatened.

A New View of Religion

Most worshipers in Russia are elderly. However, now that restrictions are off, there has been a rapid rise in church membership, and many of the new mem-

Golden Arches Over Pushkin Square

McMyasa has come to Moscow. ("Myasa" is the Russian word for meat.) More than 25,000 **applicants** lined up for jobs in Russia's first McDonald's, which opened in January of 1990. There were 660 job openings.

The McDonald's restaurant on Pushkin Square in Moscow is the fast-food company's largest operation. It seats more than 900

Two boys in Moscow get a taste of the West as they sample hamburgers and soft drinks.

January 31, 1990: a huge crowd lines up in Moscow's Pushkin Square for the official opening of the first McDonald's in the former Soviet Union.

people and serves at least 15,000 people a day. The starting wage is $2.25 an hour, high by Russian standards. About 20 percent of the applicants speak two or more languages.

The McDonald's enterprise joins a growing list of joint ventures between the United States and Russian businesses.

bers are young. Some 1,700 churches were reopened in the late 1980s, and more are being opened every year. More than 8,000 Russian Orthodox churches are open for membership, and the Russian government is once again relying on the church for support.

A Sunday evening television show is bringing religion into the homes of Russian citizens. On one show, a Russian Orthodox clergyman urged viewers: "Pause and tear yourself away from the conveyor belt of your factory, from the conveyor belt of our streets. Hear the silence that carries healing and force." Such statements would have been a crime not so long ago. Now they are soothing words for a troubled Russian populace trying to find enough to eat to stay alive.

A historic breakthrough for religion occurred in December of 1989. Then Russian leader Mikhail Gorbachev met with Polish-born Pope John Paul II in the Vatican in Rome—a first for a Soviet leader. The pope was seeking a promise of greater religious freedom and the legalization of the Ukrainian Catholic, or Uniate, church. This church was forcibly absorbed into the Russian Orthodox church in 1946. After that meeting, the Communist government began to ease its pressure on religion. Now religious orders are free to do as they please in most of the C.I.S. republics.

R E V I E W

Directions:
Number your paper from 1 to 5. Answer the following questions.
1. What two rock bands did Russian youths especially like?
2. How does the number of automobiles in Russia compare with the number in the United States?
3. What country has been most affected by the emigration of Jews from Russia?
4. Why was Gorbachev's meeting with Pope John Paul II so unusual?
5. Are there still restrictions on religions in the C.I.S.?

PART 4:
Medicine and Education

Two of the great benefits of Soviet society were free medical service and free education for all. These continue, and at the top, Russian medical practice ranks with the best in the world.

The Institute of Eye Microsurgery in Moscow leads the world in eye surgery, and people from many nations come for treatment. Russian scientists have also pioneered ultrasound techniques in the treatment of gallstones.

Medical research institutions, sanatoriums, hospitals and **polyclinics** (medical care centers for the average citizen) are run by a government ministry. The military has its own system of health care, and until the collapse of communism, there was a closed system of care for party officials and scientists.

The 2,280 sanatoriums are among the best in the world. Citizens are usually allowed to stay for 24 days while receiving care for such things as arthritis, diabetes, and hypertension. Labor unions

School children on a field trip in St. Petersburg.

traditionally controlled access to sanatoriums, but that system is breaking down as Russia and the rest of the C.I.S. change.

The great problems now are money and supplies. Medical associations in the United States and other countries have been sending equipment and supplies—including such basics as needles and bandages—to Russian hospitals. American heart specialists have been traveling to Russia to treat children with serious heart problems at no cost. Money for the project has come from private donations from all over the world. It is estimated that 40,000 children in the C.I.S. republics have heart problems that could be fatal without proper treatment. The Russian medical system is unable to handle the problem.

The C.I.S. had about 800,000 doctors in 1992, about twice that of the United States, and 2.7 million nurses and paramedics. Physician training begins right out of high school and continues for six years. Doctors in Russia do not have the same high status as those in the United States, and their salaries are not high. About 70 percent are women. Russia is also losing medical people to other countries, especially Israel, because many of the Jews who emigrated to Israel were doctors.

Literacy for the Masses

Education was a target of Lenin's Bolsheviks from the beginning. Lenin believed that literacy was necessary for the revolution in order to spread communist **ideology**. Only about one-third of the Russian population could read and write before the revolution. The literacy rate now matches that of the United States.

The Soviet school system was controlled indirectly by the Communist party and was intended to train people to serve the state. Now, with the Communist party out of the picture, the individual republics run their educational systems. However, the basic structures remain the same, and probably will be slow to change.

A Longer School Year and More Homework

Russian children begin their education in kindergarten when they become three years old. There are free daycare nurseries for children under three. Children must enter elementary school by the age of seven. The general education program lasts ten years: three years of elementary school, five of junior high, and two of secondary school. The first eight years are mandatory—that is, they must be taken—after which time all students must take a national examination. Again, the systems will begin to vary as the republics consider changes in the educational structure sometime in the future.

Under the Communist structure, all classes were rigidly regulated and there was no room for innovation on the part of students and teachers. Examinations at all levels were made up in Moscow and designed so that only the brightest children would go on beyond the 10-year education program.

Russian children go to school an average of six hours a day, six days a week. The school year is 240 days long, with no summer vacations. Instead, there are 10-day vacations in winter and spring and several one or two-day national holidays throughout the year. Russian students go to school about 60 more days a year than American children do.

Uniformity was the rule in Soviet education. That uniformity continues in Russia, but other republics are beginning

to experiment with their system. In Russia, courses of instruction and textbooks are generally the same throughout the country. Soviet schools stressed mathematics and science, and students were required to take at least five years of a foreign language. English and German continue to be the most popular. In comparison with American standards, there was little classroom discussion. Questions were usually based almost entirely on homework.

One of the strange results of the recent breakup of the Soviet Union and a turn to an open society is the lack of up-to-date history books. Many teachers are using newspaper clippings to teach with because of the rapid changes. The history books published under the direction of the Communist party were so slanted, misleading, and untruthful that

Moscow University has more than 30,000 students.

they have become useless in a society that is edging toward democracy.

Under the Communists, many students went from junior high to a labor reserve (vocational-technical) school, where they were trained for jobs in industry. Many were then assigned to industrial jobs when they graduated. Admission to Soviet specialized schools was by competitive examination. One of the weaknesses in the system was the favoritism shown to the children of Communist party officials. While this trend has slowed with the death of the party, there are still plenty of powerful former Communist officials around who can command special privileges for their children.

Students Have Choices

There was a little more flexibility in the Soviet system than appeared on the surface. Each student could choose which field of study he or she was interested in. Yet unlike the American system, which allows applications to any number of colleges, the Soviet system required most students to pick one college and one course of study. The student was generally stuck with that choice all the way through the system.

The **curriculum** in all fields was standard and a product of central planning in Moscow. It was geared toward technical skills rather than the liberal arts, which were virtually ignored.

Failing a university entrance exam continues to be a disaster for a student in the C.I.S. It means waiting a year before trying again. Many find they must turn to manual labor to survive.

R E V I E W

Directions:
Number your paper from 1 to 5. Answer the following questions.
1. What are some of the ailments a Russian citizen might receive treatment for in a sanatorium?
2. What is the percentage of women doctors in the C.I.S.?
3. Who is ahead in the literacy race, Russia or the United States?
4. At what age do Russian children begin their education?
5. What advantage did the children of Communist party officials have when it came to education?

PART 5:
Russians at Work and Play

Tempered by the cold environment and sometimes tormented by the country's harsh history, the Russian has survived to become a unique person in the modern world. He or she is at once giving to friends and suspicious of strangers. The bear hug, the kisses on the cheek, and the tears of emotion on parting are no act. Russians are both innocent and knowing. They are curious about the outside world and know that things could be better in their homeland. Russians tend to blame lazy government bureaucrats for hardships and shortages and don't mind making fun of the "bosses." There is a saying that goes around in Russian factories: "As long as the bosses pretend they are paying us a living wage, we will pretend that we are working."

The Factory System

Many outsiders thought that the Russians worked a 40-to-48 hour week, depending on the industry, in a highly organized and efficient system devised by the central planners of the former Soviet Union. Actually, they spent much more time than that at the factory because of the system they worked under.

All factories were on a **quota** system.

A newly married couple leaves flowers at a monument near St. Isaacs Cathedral in St. Petersburg.

This meant that each factory was to produce a certain number of items per month or per year. That probably would have worked had all workers filled their quotas on time. Here's how the work actually might have proceeded at the Heroic Shoe Factory in Minsk.

In June, the factory had a quota of 10,000 shoes. However, on June 1, it only had enough leather for 500 shoes, a few days' work. So the workers sat around and waited for more leather.

Chess in the park is a national pastime for many Russian citizens.

By June 20, the leather started arriving, but the workers still had 9,500 shoes to produce. So they worked long hours and on weekends, without overtime pay, to meet their quota. Quality wasn't important. The process was called **storming**, or "shhturmovshchina," where everyone entered a crash program to fulfill various quotas. This wasteful process went on in practically every factory in every industry month after month. This situation was often expressed in Russian humor. The advice of the worker was: "Don't buy anything after the 20th of the month."

This system, instituted not long after the Communists came to power, was part of the reason for the decay of the economy. Too many work hours were wasted standing around, and too many goods of poor quality were produced. The Russians are trying to reform the factory system by getting rid of central planning and turning the factories over to private enterprise, but there is resistance from old-line Communists. They want things to remain the same so that they can retain their positions of power, but it is inevitable that free enterprise will eventually win out. The economy can't grow and prosper without it.

The Russian at work is one thing. The Russian at play is another.

Russians Love the Outdoors

A common sight on a cold winter's night is a dozen men dressed in bulky clothing, their shapkas (fur hats) pulled close over their ears, trudging through the snow and into a nearby park. Some will have musical instruments clutched under their arms. Others will carry packages of food wrapped in newspaper.

They will find a clearing in the woods, start a roaring fire, break open a bottle of something to drink, and begin roasting their food on sticks over the fire. They will play their instruments and sing for hours.

It is a tribute to the Russian's traditional love of the outdoors. Even on the coldest days, couples can be seen strolling hand-in-hand along the banks of the Moscow River or ice-skating on a frozen pond. The hardier sort will head for the deep woods, even in frigid Siberia, where they will roast fish over an open fire, tell stories, and sing.

And on any day in warm or cold weather, Russians can be found on park benches, playing chess, the national game. Almost every year, a Russian Grand Master wins the world chess championship.

Music and Flowers

Just as Russians love to sing, they also love to listen to music. They will stand in line for hours for tickets to a performance. When the La Scala Opera and Chorus toured Moscow, the Russian audience was overcome with emotion, and showered the chorus with flowers.

Flowers are a special sign of affection and admiration. A Russian will arrive at someone's apartment with flowers, even if it is one flower wrapped in a newspaper. Newly married couples customarily visit nearby monuments and statues and leave flowers as part of the wedding ritual.

Russians Are Unique People

Unique means one of a kind. If something is unique, there is nothing else just like it in the world. Russians think they are unique, and sometimes even their superstitions—Russians are very **superstitious**—bear this out.

One Russian custom is to place three slips of paper under the pillow on New Year's Eve. They are labeled "Good Year," "Bad Year," and "Medium Year." In the morning, you are supposed to reach under the pillow to find out what kind of year you are going to have.

Dostoyevski, the great Russian author, wrote that Russians were half saint, half savage. He attributed this to their harsh heritage.

The **babushkas** (grandmothers) are interesting characters. They seem to be everywhere: pushing into lines, instructing people on how to behave, or spoiling their grandchildren like grandmothers everywhere.

An American journalist recalls being asked by Russian friends to dinner at their apartment. On the way in, he passed a babushka, guardian of the apartment house.

"Who is he?" she demanded sharply, pointing to the journalist and blocking the door. "What is he doing here? Where are his papers? I must see his papers." All this of people she had known for years!

The same woman might caution a stranger to bundle up against the wind, then follow him to make sure he does. Or she could tell another stranger his dog is out of place in a park. "This is state property and it's against the law," she might say.

Nonetheless, Russians believe themselves to be the most kind-hearted people in the world, and many would agree.

A writer called the Russian Embassy one day to ask questions about the new Russian government under Boris Yeltsin. A man with a hoarse voice and a thick accent answered the phone. When the writer stated his business, the man on the other end of the phone immediately raised his voice and greeted him like an old friend.

"Your name is GeoRGE Smith-WICK," he half-shouted, placing emphasis on the name as though the writer was Lenin brought back to life. "GeoRGE SmithWICK, my friend. What can I do for you. Anything at ALL." And sure enough, he spent 20 minutes answering the writer's questions in rapid-fire manner, revealing yet another unique Russian trait. Half the answers were wrong, but the man was so anxious to please his questioner that he gave answers whether he understood the question or not.

REVIEW

Directions:
Number your paper from 1 to 5. Answer the following questions.
1. What is a quota system?
2. What does **storming** mean, and why was it so damaging to the economy of the former Soviet Union?
3. What are some of the activities that a Russian man might do on a night out on the town?
4. How do Russian citizens use flowers as a sign of admiration and affection?
5. What are babushkas? How do they treat strangers?

PART 6:
Looking Ahead

There is no way to predict with any certainty the course of the Commonwealth of Independent States and its giant leader, Russia, in the years ahead. There is too much turmoil and uncertainty as the Commonwealth slowly makes the shift from a planned to a market economy. And then there is the nationality problem. The republics of the former Soviet Union had many different **ethnic** backgrounds. The people of each republic had little in common with members of the other republics.

Mikhail Gefter, a retired historian who nows spends his days reading and writing in the sun outside his dacha near Moscow, made an uncannily accurate prediction about the future of the Soviet Union in 1990, two years before the final breakup of the Soviet Union.

"The nationalities, not the economy, are Gorbachev's biggest problem," he said in referring to the leader of the Soviet Union at the time. Gefter said he thought the Soviet Union would become a loose federation of semi-autonomous national republics. He was almost exactly right, except that the republics did not become semi-autonomous; they became completely independent, with only the thin thread of the C.I.S. holding 11 of the 15 former Soviet republics together.

"The Mongols originally created this monstrous empire," Gefter said, "and the Russians just took it over. There's been nothing but trouble since."

The trouble continues, with Christian Armenia and Muslim Azerbaijan actually at war over a disputed territory, Nagorno-Karabakh. The Muslims are discontented in the southwest, and various parts of Russia are seeking to secede and create even more independent republics. The Commonwealth, at the instigation of Russia, is considering forming an armed force to keep the peace among the republics in much the same way the United Nations attempts to keep the peace worldwide.

Many Questions

Now people wonder whether order can be restored without the republics returning to dictatorship, and there are those who are actively trying to bring this about. After a thousand years of varying degrees of totalitarian rule, the people of Russia and the other republics are finding it difficult to adjust to the new freedoms and forget the old hatreds. There are always people around willing to take advantage of the confusion and trying to seize power.

Making it even more difficult is the miserable mess left by the Communist party, not only in the economy, but in the environment and in agriculture. High inflation, a sharply rising crime rate (up 30 percent in 1992 alone), a growing alcohol and drug problem, and a power struggle between the Russian parliament and President Boris Yeltsin con-

To combat the declining birth rate in Russian cities in the western part of the country, the government encourages women to marry and have many children. Continuous weddings are held in wedding palaces like this one all over the country.

tributed to the despair of those who longed for peace, security, and complete freedom in 1992.

Here is one woman's feelings about the condition of Russia today and her view of the future. Amy Tatko is a history student at Irkutsk State University in Irkutsk, a large Siberian city.

"I love Russia, but Irkutsk is one of the most dirty, wretched, uncivilized places on our planet. In inhumanly crowded public transportation, struggling to get enough to eat, and horrified by the way men treat women, I nonetheless found a better side to the Russians: strength, determination, and a love of truth. A real democracy may one day rise from the ash of the Soviet regime," Ms. Tatko said.

"The people of my generation, those in their teens and twenties, seem hard hit. Raised and educated on Communist **propaganda**, which many of them believed, they are now denied a past and don't see a future. Their parents' **generation** must provide the wisdom and strength to guide Russia into a new era," she said.

"A common understanding of middle-aged Russians is that they must tighten their wallets, rethink their budgets, and prepare for a long, hard journey to a democratic future—a future they may not live to see, but must obtain for their children and grandchildren.

"There is growing crime, empty shelves, rising prices, sick and dying children, and an absence of governmental control or **ideology**. But the dreams of the people seem genuine; and it is from dreams that progress, ideals, and new beginnings often spring.

"Nothing equals the most basic human desires for freedom, a safe future, and a better life. Everything is horrible! I never imagined it would get so bad, but I also never imagined such progress and freedom. We are wearing the clothes we always wanted to, criticizing the leaders and system we always despised, watching foreign films and experiencing other cultures, and talking and dreaming about absolutely anything we want. I'd never go back," she said.

Inequality in a Classless Society

There are many problems left over from the Communist regime that will not go away. Communist doctrine called for a classless society, but a ruling **elite** existed in the Soviet Union and this elite lived much better than the average citizen. There was also inequality between men and women and among the different nationalities and cultural groups. According to Marxist **theory**, inequality and a powerful ruling class were prod-

Many of the 660 employees who work at Moscow's first McDonald's are women. McDonald's wages are high by Soviet standards.

ucts of capitalism and should not be found in a communist society. He was wrong, because he overlooked the ways of human nature.

Until the breakup of the Soviet Union in December 1991, most of the power, privileges, and luxuries in the country belonged to a very small group of the ruling elite. The group included party leaders, top government officials, military leaders and industrial managers, as well as leading scientists, athletes, and entertainment personalities. With few exceptions, they were party members.

Members of this group found more places to spend their money; they were allowed to shop in special stores and could travel outside the country. Other advantages included better housing, medical care, and vacation homes. Their children had an easier time getting into

Moscow, February 4, 1990: A man attending a huge demonstration for democracy strains to hear someone giving a speech. The rally, which called for adopting a multi-party system in the Soviet Union, was probably the largest demonstration to take place in Moscow since 1917.

universities, the **Komsomol**, and the party itself. Boris Yeltsin, when he was first elected president of Russia, was embarrassed to discover that a large home, several servants, a swimming pool, and tennis courts went with the office.

Now, these former Communist leaders are fighting to keep their privileges, and they form the hard core of opposition to democracy.

Russian Women

Women were instrumental in building the Soviet economy over the years. In the 1930s and 1940s, large numbers of women entered a work force that was severely drained by Stalin's purges and World War II. Today, female labor is still very important to the economy. Almost all women work, and they make up half the Commonwealth work force.

Even so, Russian women have achieved only limited equality. Although they belong to many different professions, they are seldom able to rise to the top of them. Few women held important government or party offices in the Soviet Union. The average woman makes only about 65 percent as much as her male counterpart, about the same as women in the United States. But in the United States, the government and the courts have narrowed this gap considerably in the last several years.

Sexual inequality continues at home. In traditional Russian families, the women are expected to run the household. Few Russian husbands will share the housework with their working wives. The woman must take care of the children, clean the house, and fix the meals. Women also do the shopping, which means waiting in line for hours. In effect, a majority of Russian women have to perform two full-time jobs, one as a wage-earner and the other as a homemaker. While this may be similar to what is happening in Western countries, resources are so short in Russia that the problems for the average woman are multiplied.

This double burden is having a drastic effect on the size of Russian families.

Many women do not want more than one child. As a result, population growth, especially in western Russia, is dropping rapidly, despite government efforts to encourage women to have more children. Among Muslims in the poorer southern republics, the birth rate has been increasing rapidly.

Surprise will continue to be the norm as the Commonwealth and Russia move toward the twenty-first century.

R E V I E W

Directions:
Number your paper from 1 to 5. Answer the following questions.
1. What did historian Mikhail Gefter say was the biggest problem with the former Soviet Union?
2. How were women instrumental in building the Soviet economy?
3. What embarrassment did Boris Yeltsin face when he became president of Russia?
4. Name an area of Russian society where inequality exists?
5. Why are Russian women not having as many children as they used to have?

<u>MAP SKILLS</u>

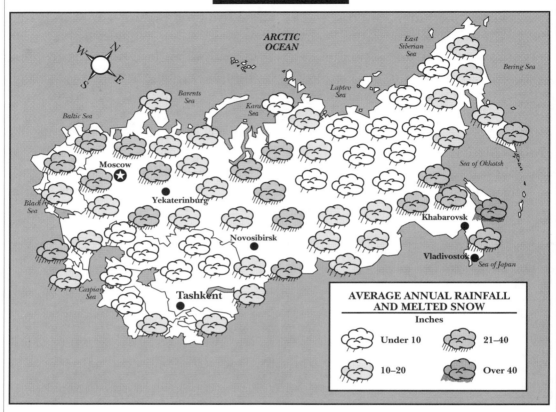

AVERAGE ANNUAL PRECIPITATION IN THE C.I.S.

This map uses different symbols to show how much precipitation (rain and snow) usually falls in the course of a year in the C.I.S. Look at the map legend to find out what these symbols mean.

Directions: Answer the following questions using the map on this page.

1. Near what sea does it rain more than 40 inches a year?
2. How many inches of rain and melted snow does Moscow get each year?
3. How much rain falls east of the Caspian Sea each year?
4. Is there more precipitation in the northeastern or northwestern part of the C.I.S.?
5. On the average, how much rain and snow fall in and around Novosibirsk each year?
6. Does Novosibirsk get more or less precipitation than Vladivostok?
7. How much precipitation does Vladivostok get as compared with Moscow?

CHAPTER 6 REVIEW

Summary of Life Today

Change has come rapidly to the former Soviet Union since its breakup in December 1991. Prices have risen; there are fewer goods and less food. And the fight for freedom of expression continues as former Communist party members oppose the march toward democracy. The new freedoms continue to grow nonetheless, and television programs are now bringing reality and free political discussion to the Russian people. Life is hard for the average Russian family because of food shortages and the lack of adequate housing.

Western culture has made a big impact in Russia, especially with the young. Rock music and jeans are popular, and young people are learning Western ways from television.

Religion, now that it is free of restrictions imposed by the Communist party, is making a comeback, and more churches are reopening yearly. Russian Jewry has benefited from the changes. Many have emigrated to Israel for a new way of life.

Medical care and education for all was a major goal of the Communist party, and 99 percent of Russians can read and write. The medical program has suffered from lack of money and supplies, and Western nations are helping out.

Russians are a vital, warm people, suspicious of strangers but loving of their friends and family. The old Communist factory system lingers on in parts of the Commonwealth as the various republics struggle to change from a planned, central economy to a market economy. Part of the Russian lifestyle is love of the outdoors, and they will go outdoors for hours even in the coldest weather.

There is no way to predict with any certainty the course of events in the former Soviet Union as the now-independent republics struggle to find their way to prosperity and peace. Many problems were left behind by the Communist party and by the very nature of the nationality makeup of the Soviet Union. Fighting broke out between some of the republics, and the Commonwealth has considered forming an armed force to keep the peace.

Russian women have to work and run their household, with little help from their husbands. One result of this has been a declining birth rate.

Critical Thinking Skills

Directions: Give some serious thought to these questions. Answer in complete sentences.

1. Who created collective farms? Why were they created?
2. In what field of medicine does Russia excel?
3. What are babushkas and why are they interesting?
4. Compare the equality of women in Russia with that of women in the United States.

For Discussion

Directions: Discuss these questions with your class. Appoint one class member to write the ideas you discover on the board.

1. If it were up to you, would you rather have all the food you could eat or all the freedom you want?
2. How important is religious freedom to you?
3. Do you think the Russian people are better off with—or without—communism?
4. Try to predict the future of the Commonwealth of Independent States. Do you think democracy will survive?

Write It!

Directions: Write a letter to Boris Yeltsin, president of Russia. In it, express your thoughts about democracy and what it has meant to you as a citizen of the United States.

For You to Do

Directions: Invite an expert on Russia from a local college or university, or even from your own school, to your classroom to discuss the many changes occurring in Russia. Make a list of questions you would like to ask this expert.

GLOSSARY

abdicate—to cast off, discard; to step down from a position of power

absolute—total, complete

access—the right to enter, approach, or use

aggressive—combative, forceful

agriculture—the science or art of growing crops and raising animals for food

applicant—a person who makes a request in writing, as for a job or to enter a university

architecture—a special style of designing buildings

arid—dry; not having enough rainfall to grow crops

armistice—an agreement to stop fighting during a war

artifact—a man-made object representing a culture

assassination—murder by sudden attack, often for political reasons

autonomous—self-governing

babushka—the Russian word for "grandmother"

ballet—a dance whose movements tell a story

Bloody Sunday—refers to Sunday, January 22, 1905, when a huge, but peaceful crowd was gunned down by the tsar's cossack cavalry; the crowd was bringing a petition to Tsar Nicholas II asking for more freedom

bog—a poorly drained area of wet, spongy ground

borscht—an Eastern European soup or stew that is popular in the former Soviet Union

boyars—the wealthy landowners or noble class that existed in Russia until the time of Peter the Great

bureaucracy—layers of government that generally administer day-to-day activities

calculation—a method of figuring something out

capitalist—referring to an economic system or a person who believes in an economic system that features private ownership of property and the means of production, whereby the production, distribution, and prices of goods are determined by the free market

catacombs—underground vaults or tunnels

Central Committee—an organization chosen from the ranks of the All-Union Party Congress that met twice a year to carry on the work of the Communist party between congresses; elected the General Secretary, as well as members of the Politburo and the Secretariat

checks and balances—referring to the system of government in the U.S., in which the three branches of government (legislative, executive and judicial) act as "checks" and "balances" on one another, so that no single branch of government can gain absolute control

chernozem—rich, fertile, black soil

circumference—the line bounding a circle; the external boundary or surface of an object

climate—the average weather conditions of a region

cold war—starting after World War II, a long period of tension and hostility between the United States and the Soviet Union that never led to direct military confrontation between them

collective—in communist countries, a huge farm owned by the government

commerce—trade among people or nations

complex—not simple; complicated

conditioned reflex—a learned response in which one message received from the environment takes the place of another

Congress of People's Deputies—an organization elected by the people that meets at least once a year to set policy and review the activities of the Supreme Soviet

constitution—a basic document that says how a country should be governed

constitutional—belonging to, or inherent in, the constitution

continent—a large land division on the Earth

contrast—the differences between one thing and another

converted—changed over

coronation—the ceremony in which a monarch is crowned

cosmonaut—a Russian astronaut; the Russian word for astronaut

cultivate—prepare the soil for crops

culture—the beliefs and customs of a racial or ethnic group

curriculum—a fixed series of studies

customs—a common or usual practice

dacha—in the C.I.S., a vacation home or home in the country

diverse—different, varied

document—anything printed or written that is relied upon to make a record of or prove something

domination—the state of having command or control over people or events

edict—an authoratative order or decision; a decree

elaborate—worked out carefully and in great detail

elegant—dignified and graceful

elite—a small but often powerful or important group of people

emigrate—to leave one country for another

enclave—an area surrounded by another area that is completely different in some way, such as in ethnic population

environment—everything around us, including land, air, our homes, and family

ethnic—relating to certain racial or cultural groups

exile—forced removal from one's home or country

famine—a food shortage that causes starvation

fertile—rich; refers to land that is able to grow crops

generation—the average period, about 30 years, between the birth of one group and the birth of its children

glaciers—large, slowly moving masses of ice and snow

glasnost—a Russian word meaning "openness"; Soviet President Mikhail Gorbachev's policy of dealing openly and honestly with everyone

Great Purge—Stalin's public program of terror in the mid-1930s when millions of people were killed or sent to labor camps because they were suspected of being political enemies

heritage—things that are handed down from the previous generation

humid—moist

icon—a religious object; a religious image usually painted on a small wooden panel; a religious painting

ideology—a way of thinking about life or culture

immigrant—someone who comes into one country from another country

infiltration—entering into somewhere or something gradually

irrigation—a method of supplying water to land by ditches, pipes, or wells

Kara Kum—a desert region in the Soviet republic of Turkmenistan that is the driest area in the C.I.S.

Komsomol—a disbanded Communist youth organization whose members were between the ages of 14 and 28

legacy—something that is inherited

legislature—a lawmaking body

liberal—generous; also, broad-minded in political matters

livestock—farm animals

manifesto—a public declaration of intentions or views

market—the rate or price being offered for something based on the demand for it

market economy—a system that exists in capitalist countries where property and the means of production are privately owned, and the production, distribution, and pricing of goods depends upon supply and demand

massacre—the cruel killing of large numbers of people or animals; mass murder

method acting—a realistic style of acting invented by Konstantin Stanislavsky

milestone—an important point in life or in the course of events

moats—water-filled ditches around a castle, used for defense

monarch—a king, queen, or tsar

moors—open uncultivated areas with poor soil; usually covered by grass and small shrubs

museum—a place where art, historical objects, and other things of value are displayed

Nobel Prize—an international prize awarded every year for writing, for promoting peace, and in the various sciences

nomads—groups of people who move from place to place in search of food

oasis—a fertile place in a desert; the plural form is "oases"

obedience—the act or state of agreeing to follow, or submit to, an authority

October Manifesto—a public declaration made by Tsar Nicholas II on October 30, 1905 promising the Russian people greater freedom and a parliament

opera—a type of play created in Italy that is sung instead of spoken

GLOSSARY

pampered—treated with a great deal of care and attention

parcel—to divide into parts, give out, or distribute

partisan—favorable to; a member of a guerrilla band or a small number of troops operating behind enemy lines

party line—a term used to describe the official policy of the Communist party

peaceful coexistence—Soviet leader Nikita Khrushchev's policy that stated that the Soviet Union and the United States could still compete against each other but avoid war

peat bogs—low, wet regions in which peat, a decaying organic material, is found

pension—a sum of money paid regularly to a retired worker

people's assessors—judge's assistants who are not required to have any legal training and are not paid; could be considered a substitute for a jury, since Soviet courts do not have a jury system

perestroika—a Russian word meaning "restructuring"; Soviet President Mikhail Gorbachev's program of political and economic reforms

permafrost—ground that is frozen all the time

philosopher—one who pursues wisdom, and has ideas about learning, thinking, and the way life works

planned economy—a system in which the government controls all property and means of production, and can decide how much to produce, how to distribute it, and what prices to charge, etc.

plateau—a large area of flat land that sits high above the surrounding land

pogroms—riots aimed against Jews, involving vandalism and murder

Politburo—the policy-making body of the Communist party

polyclinics—medical care centers for average citizens

predominant—something that is more important or noticeable in a particular setting

prone—tending to do something; vulnerable or susceptible to something

propaganda—the spreading of news or ideas, whether true or not

quota—an assigned amount of work that must be met or completed within a certain amount of time

radical—extreme; a person who takes an extreme viewpoint

research—inquiry, examination, or investigation; the collecting of information on a particular subject

resurgence—the act or state of coming back strongly

ruble—the monetary unit of the C.I.S.

Russification—a program by which the Soviet government tried to impose Russian language and government on other national groups in the country, such as the Baltic states of Estonia, Lithuania, and Latvia

satellite—an object intended to orbit the Earth

shapka—a Russian fur hat

shrine—a holy place

Solidarity—in Poland, an organization of the free trade unions

soviet—a Russian word meaning "council"

sputnik—a Russian word meaning "satellite" or literally, "traveling companion"

steppe—a grassy plain in the Soviet Union that resembles flat prairie country in the American Midwest

storming—a crash program to fulfill quotas

structured—the way something is made up; its form; something that is arranged in a definite and often rigid pattern of organization

superpower—a very powerful nation, such as the Soviet Union or the United States after World War II

superstitious—believing in something that cannot be proved by known laws of science

Supreme Soviet—Russia's full-time legislature consisting of two houses of equal power

taiga—a Russian word meaning "thick forest"

terrain—the physical features of a piece of land

theory—an idea or plan on how something should be done

tradition—a custom that has continued for many years

transfixed—to become motionless

tsars—the monarchs who ruled Russia prior to the Bolshevik Revolution in 1917

tundra—flat northern land, usually frozen, with little vegetation

uniformity—the condition of always being the same; standardization

universal—world-wide

wilderness—an area of land that is not farmed and has few people living on it; usually overgrown with vegetation

Young Octobrists—a disbanded Communist youth organization whose members were between the ages of seven and nine

Young Pioneers—a disbanded Communist youth organization whose members were between the ages of nine and fourteen

zakaz—a package of food low-ranking Communist party members received monthly as a special privilege in the former Soviet Union

INDEX

INDEX